Easy
entertaining

easy
entertaining

easy entertaining

simple recipes for every occasion

RYLAND
PETERS
& SMALL

LONDON NEW YORK

Designer Sarah Fraser
Editor Sharon Ashman
Production Deborah Wehner
Art Director Gabriella Le Grazie
Publishing Director Alison Starling

Index Hilary Bird

First published in Great Britain
in 2004
by Ryland Peters & Small
20–21 Jockey's Fields
London WC1R 4BW
www.rylandpeters.com

10 9 8 7 6 5 4 3 2

ISBN 1 84172 573 0

Printed in China

A CIP catalogue record for this book is
available from the British Library.

Notes
All spoon measurements are level
unless otherwise specified.

Ovens should be preheated to the
specified temperature. If using a
fan-assisted oven, cooking times
should be reduced according to the
manufacturer's instructions.

Uncooked or partly cooked eggs should
not be served to the very young, the
very old or frail, or to pregnant women.

Specialist Asian ingredients are
available in larger supermarkets and
Asian stores.

To sterilize preserving jars, wash them
in hot, soapy water and rinse in boiling
water. Place in a large saucepan and
then cover with hot water. With the
saucepan lid on, bring the water to
the boil and continue boiling for
15 minutes. Turn off the heat, then
leave the jars in the hot water until just
before they are to be filled. Drain and
dry. Sterilize the lids for 5 minutes,
by boiling, or according to the
manufacturer's instructions. Jars
should be filled and sealed while
they are still hot.

contents

introduction

Entertaining can take many forms but the most important thing to bear in mind is that everyone should enjoy themselves – and that includes you, the cook. Whether you are planning a summer garden party or a quiet lunch for a close friend, arranging a smart dinner party or a casual weekend brunch, this book has a huge selection of recipe suggestions to suit. Throughout, the emphasis is on 'easy', but this in no way compromises the food you can cook, its taste or the 'wow' factor. Here you will find a full range of dishes from around the world that will inspire you to create wonderful meals for your guests using only the freshest and tastiest ingredients.

Each recipe is presented in easy-to-follow stages to make your time in the kitchen as simple and as stress-free as possible. You will soon find yourself delving enthusiastically into the book's different chapters to come up with menus to suit your own culinary gatherings and the tastes of your guests. You will be amazed at the way entertaining can play such a pleasurable part in your social life.

So, don't waste any more time. Invite some friends round now and get reading – there's entertaining to be done!

brunch

american pancakes

A stack of fluffy, American-style pancakes in the morning will keep you and your guests fuelled for hours. Make the batter before bedtime and leave it overnight in the fridge. In the morning, you'll have a brunch feast in minutes.

250 g plain flour
2 teaspoons baking powder
1 teaspoon sea salt
3 tablespoons sugar
250 ml milk
2 eggs, lightly beaten
50 g unsalted butter, melted, plus extra for cooking

maple butter syrup

80 ml maple syrup
25 g unsalted butter

makes 8–12, serves 4

Sift the flour, baking powder, salt and sugar into a bowl. Mix the milk, eggs and the 50 g melted butter in a large jug, then add the flour mixture and mix quickly to make a batter (don't worry about lumps – they're good). Alternatively, make the batter in a bowl and transfer to a jug.

Heat a cast-iron frying pan or flat-surfaced griddle until medium hot. Grease lightly with extra butter, then pour in the batter in batches to make rounds 8–10 cm in diameter. Cook for 1–2 minutes or until bubbles form on top of the pancakes and the underside is golden, then flip each one over and cook for 1 minute more. Keep the pancakes warm in a low oven while you cook the remaining batches.

Heat the maple syrup and butter together in a small saucepan or microwave until the butter is melted. Stack the pancakes on warmed plates and pour over the buttery syrup.

A classic brunch dish with a twist! If you don't have a waffle iron, simply drop a ladle of batter onto a lightly greased, heated frying pan and fry until golden on both sides.

waffles with maple syrup ice cream

ice cream

500 ml double cream

250 ml milk

seeds from 1 vanilla pod

5 egg yolks

125 ml maple syrup

waffles

150 g plain flour

1 teaspoon baking powder

½ teaspoon
bicarbonate of soda

1 tablespoon caster sugar

125 ml buttermilk

1 egg, lightly beaten

75 g butter, melted

maple syrup, to serve

waffle iron, lightly greased

serves 6

To make the ice cream, put the cream, milk and vanilla seeds in a saucepan and heat until the mixture reaches boiling point. Remove the pan from the heat and set aside.

Meanwhile, put the egg yolks and maple syrup in a bowl and beat. Stir in the heated cream mixture and return to the pan. Heat gently, stirring, until the mixture thickens enough to coat the back of a wooden spoon. Do not boil or the mixture will curdle. Remove from the heat and let cool. Freeze in an ice cream maker, following the manufacturer's instructions. If you don't have an ice cream maker, pour the mixture into flat freezer trays and put them in the freezer. Let the mixture partially freeze, then beat to break up the ice crystals and return the trays to the freezer. Repeat several times – the more you do it, the smoother the end result.

To make the waffles, sift the flour, baking powder and bicarbonate of soda into a bowl. Stir in the sugar. Put the buttermilk, egg and melted butter in a second bowl and beat well. Beat into the dry ingredients until you have a smooth batter.

Spoon a layer of the batter into a heated waffle iron and spread flat. Cook for about 1 minute until crisp and golden. Serve hot with a scoop of ice cream and a little extra maple syrup.

pecan and chocolate **muffins**

250 g self-raising flour

1 teaspoon baking powder

75 g pecan nuts, finely ground

125 g soft brown sugar

1 egg

50 ml maple syrup

250 ml milk

50 g butter, melted

100 g dark chocolate, coarsely chopped into very small pieces

chopped pecans, to decorate

a 12-hole muffin tray, lined with paper cases

makes 12

Use good-quality dark chocolate, chopped up, rather than chocolate chips, as it has a much better flavour and texture.

Sift the flour and baking powder into a bowl and stir in the pecan nuts and sugar. Put the egg, maple syrup, milk and melted butter in a second bowl and beat well. Beat into the dry ingredients, then fold in the chocolate pieces.

Spoon the mixture into the paper cases, sprinkling the surface with extra chopped pecans.

Bake in a preheated oven at 200°C (400°F) Gas 6 for 18–20 minutes until risen and golden. Cool on a wire tray and serve warm.

This recipe is for two simply because it's not easy to cook more than this quantity at a time. Make separate batches if there are more than two of you. If you can find wild mushrooms such as girolles or chanterelles to use instead, you're in for a real treat.

scrambled eggs with mushrooms

250 g portobello mushrooms,
or mixed wild mushrooms

6 free range eggs

50 g unsalted butter

2 teaspoons chopped fresh thyme leaves

sea salt and freshly ground black pepper

to serve

fresh thyme leaves

toast

sautéed mushrooms (optional)

serves 2

Wipe the mushrooms with a damp cloth and cut into thick slices. Put the eggs in a bowl, add salt and pepper to taste and beat until blended.

Melt 40 g of the butter in a large frying pan. As soon as it stops foaming, add the mushrooms, thyme, salt and pepper. Fry over medium heat until lightly browned and the juices begin to run.

Push the mushrooms to one side of the pan, add the remaining butter, then pour in the beaten eggs, stirring with a fork until almost set.

Gradually stir in the mushrooms from the sides of the pan, cook a moment longer, then spoon onto serving plates. Sprinkle with thyme leaves and serve with toast and a few extra sautéed mushrooms, if using.

eggs benedict

If you fry the Parma ham it becomes really crisp, adding a lovely texture to the creamy sauce and egg yolks. Try replacing the ham with smoked salmon or, if you have vegetarian guests, wilted spinach.

4 large slices of Parma ham

4 free range eggs

1–2 tablespoons vinegar, preferably distilled

4 plain English muffins

hollandaise sauce

250 g unsalted butter

3 free range egg yolks

2 tablespoons water

1 teaspoon freshly squeezed lemon juice

sea salt and cracked black pepper

serves 4

To make the hollandaise sauce, put the butter in a small saucepan and melt gently over very low heat, without letting it brown. Put the egg yolks, water and lemon juice in a blender and process until frothy. With the blade turning, gradually pour in the melted butter in a steady stream until the sauce is thickened and glossy. Transfer the sauce to a bowl set over a saucepan of hot water. Cover and keep the sauce warm.

Grill or fry the slices of Parma ham until really crisp and keep them warm in a low oven. To poach the eggs, bring a saucepan of lightly salted water to the boil. Add the vinegar and reduce to a gentle simmer. Swirl the water well with a fork and crack 2 eggs into the water. Cook for 3 minutes, remove with a slotted spoon and keep warm in a low oven. Repeat with the remaining 2 eggs.

Meanwhile, toast the muffins whole and top each one with a slice of crispy ham. Put a poached egg on top of the ham. Spoon over the hollandaise sauce, season with salt and pepper and serve at once.

french toast
with smoky bacon and spiked tomatoes

Day-old bread is best for this recipe as it will soak up more of the eggy mixture and fry better than fresh bread. The eggs make the bread puff up inside like a delicious soufflé.

Preheat the grill. Put the eggs in a bowl and beat until blended. Add plenty of salt and pepper. Pour into a large, shallow dish, then dip the slices of bread in the egg mixture, coating them all over, then set the dish aside for a few minutes to let the egg soak into the bread.

Meanwhile, grill the bacon for 1–2 minutes on each side until crisp. Transfer to a low oven to keep it warm.

Heat 1 tablespoon of the olive oil in a frying pan until hot. Add the tomatoes and sprinkle with the sugar. Fry for 1–2 minutes on each side until caramelized. Sprinkle with the chilli oil and remove from the heat. Transfer to a plate and put in a very low oven to keep warm.

Wipe the frying pan clean with kitchen paper, add the butter and remaining oil and heat until hot. Add the egg-soaked bread, in batches if necessary, and fry for 2 minutes on each side until crisp and golden.

Put 2 triangles on each plate with 3 pieces of bacon on top. Spoon the tomatoes over the bacon, sprinkle with the basil and serve immediately.

4 eggs

4 slices thick white bread, halved diagonally

12 slices of smoked streaky bacon

2 tablespoons olive oil

4 large plum tomatoes, halved lengthways

2 teaspoons sugar

2 teaspoons chilli oil

25 g butter

2 tablespoons basil leaves, torn

sea salt and freshly ground black pepper

serves 4

warm potato tortilla
with smoked salmon

Tortillas make a great base for serving smoked salmon and eggs at a special brunch. You can make individual tortillas in little blini pans (sold in good kitchenware shops), but the dish is equally delicious when the tortilla is cooked in a large frying pan and cut into wedges.

400 g small, waxy, salad-style potatoes

25 g butter

1 small onion, sliced

4 eggs

250 g smoked salmon

sea salt and freshly ground black pepper

to serve

smoked salmon

salmon caviar (*keta*)

crème fraîche

4 blini pans (optional)

serves 4

Cook the potatoes in a saucepan of lightly salted, boiling water for 10–12 minutes until cooked but not falling apart. Drain and refresh under cold water. Pat dry and cut into small cubes.

Put half the butter in a frying pan, melt gently, add the onion and cook gently for 5 minutes. Add the cubed potatoes and cook for a further 5 minutes.

Put the eggs, salt and pepper in a bowl. Beat well, then stir in the potato and onion mixture. Put the remaining butter into 4 blini pans or 1 frying pan, then add the egg mixture.

Cook over gentle heat for 6–8 minutes, then flip the tortilla or transfer to a preheated grill to set and lightly brown the top. If you are making 1 large tortilla, cook it for about 10 minutes before grilling.

Let cool a little, then serve topped with smoked salmon, a little salmon caviar and a dollop of crème fraîche.

starters

baked chèvre

Simple and delicious, this can be served as a starter or whipped up as a quick lunchtime snack for unexpected guests.

4 thick slices of chèvre cheese with rind, 50 g per serving

extra virgin olive oil, for sprinkling

1 tablespoon chopped fresh thyme leaves

freshly ground black pepper

to serve

4 slices of sourdough bread

1–2 garlic cloves, halved

green salad

a baking sheet, lined with foil

serves 4

Put the chèvre slices onto the prepared baking sheet, sprinkle with a little oil, dot with thyme leaves and season with pepper. Bake in a preheated oven at 200°C (400°F) Gas 6 for 10-12 minutes until just starting to ooze and run.

Meanwhile, toast the sourdough and rub it with the cut garlic. When the cheese is ready, spread it onto the toasted, garlicky sourdough and serve with a green salad.

lemon potato latkes
with gingered avocado crème

2 large potatoes, about 750 g

1 small onion, finely chopped

grated zest of 1 unwaxed lemon

2 teaspoons freshly squeezed lemon juice

4 tablespoons plain flour

¼ teaspoon baking powder

1 teaspoon sea salt

olive oil, for frying

gingered avocado crème

1 large ripe avocado, halved and stoned

freshly squeezed juice of 1 lime

1–2 teaspoons finely grated ginger

½ teaspoon crushed garlic

1 red chilli, deseeded and finely chopped, or 1 tablespoon chilli sauce

1 tablespoon light soy sauce

2 tablespoons thick plain yoghurt

makes 20–24, serves 4

Though rather indulgent, fried potato cakes are worth every wicked mouthful. Keep them small and they'll cook in minutes. Eat them straight away or reheat in a hot oven for five minutes.

To make the latkes, peel the potatoes, then grate on the coarse side of a box grater or in a food processor. Transfer to a sieve and let drain. Press excess moisture out of the potatoes (or they will 'spit' when fried) and put them in a bowl. Add the onion, the lemon zest and juice, flour, baking powder and salt and mix well. Return to the sieve – liquid will continue to drain out of the mixture while you prepare to cook the latkes.

Heat about 5 mm depth of olive oil in a large frying pan. Add rounded tablespoons of the mixture to the pan and flatten slightly; don't overcrowd the pan. Fry for 2–3 minutes on each side until golden and crisp. Remove with a slotted spoon and drain on kitchen paper. Keep the latkes warm in a low oven while you cook the remaining batches.

To make the avocado crème, scoop the avocado flesh into a bowl and mash with a fork. Add the remaining ingredients and beat until smooth. Serve with the latkes.

This makes an elegant first course to serve to friends. The cream has a punchy pepper kick to it, with cool lemon undertones. Tossing the salmon in the dill gives it a lovely fresh appearance.

smoked salmon crostini

250 g thinly sliced smoked salmon

2 tablespoons chopped fresh dill

sea salt

crostini

1 Italian sfilatino* or thin French baguette, thinly sliced diagonally

extra virgin olive oil, for brushing

lemon pepper cream

2 teaspoons black peppercorns

75 ml mascarpone cheese

75 ml milk

finely grated zest and juice of 1 unwaxed lemon

a baking sheet

serves 6

*A sfilatino is a long, thin loaf available from Italian delicatessens and larger supermarkets.

To make the crostini, brush both sides of each slice of bread with olive oil and spread out on a baking sheet. Bake in a preheated oven at 190°C (375°F) Gas 5 for about 10 minutes until crisp and golden. Let cool, then keep in an airtight container until ready to use. It is best to reheat them in the oven before adding the topping.

To make the lemon pepper cream, pound or grind the peppercorns as finely as possible. Beat the mascarpone with the ground pepper, add the milk and lemon zest and beat again. Season with salt and lemon juice to taste. Chill until needed.

Toss the smoked salmon with the chopped dill. Spread the crostini with the lemon pepper cream and put a mound of smoked salmon on top. Squeeze over a little more lemon juice and serve immediately.

grilled polenta with grilled peppers

This recipe uses quick-cook polenta to save time. You can prepare the polenta and the basil oil the day before, leaving you very little to do when your guests arrive.

1 packet quick-cook polenta, about 100 g

2 tablespoons butter

olive oil, for brushing

sea salt and freshly ground black pepper

sprigs of basil and oregano, to serve

basil oil

1 large bunch of basil

125 ml extra virgin olive oil

char-grilled peppers

6 red or yellow peppers, preferably long peppers,
halved and deseeded

olive oil, for coating

a springform cake tin, oiled

serves 8

Prepare the polenta according to the packet instructions, stir in the butter, then pour into the prepared cake tin. Let cool and set. Chill until ready to grill.

To make the basil oil, put the basil in a food processor and pulse until finely chopped. Add the oil gradually through the feed tube, then add a pinch of salt. Chill in the refrigerator for at least 30 minutes, or preferably overnight to intensify the flavour and colour. Strain through a nylon sieve or a tea strainer into a jug.

To cook the peppers, put the halves or pieces in a plastic bag, add the olive oil, salt and pepper and shake to coat with oil. Heat a stove-top grill pan over medium heat until hot. Remove the peppers from the bag and put them, skin side down, on the pan. Put a heavy weight, such as a large saucepan, on top and cook until dark and charred with marks. Turn the pieces over, put the saucepan back on top and cook until tender. Use as they are or, to remove the skins, transfer the peppers to a small saucepan and cover with the lid – the skins will gently steam off and you won't lose any of the delicious juices.

Turn the polenta out of the cake tin and cut into 8 wedges. Reheat the grill pan, then brush the polenta wedges with olive oil, put them in the pan and cook until barred with brown on one side. Turn the pieces over and cook the other side until hot, golden and browned. Transfer to warm serving plates, top with the peppers, drizzle with basil oil and any pepper juices, add basil and oregano sprigs and serve.

prawns with parsley and lemon

Prawns are very popular as a starter. Some of them are striped grey or blue; others have silvery shells or look pink or translucent. This recipe suits almost any prawn variety – adjust the cooking time to suit the size. Tails alone cook more quickly than whole prawns.

750 g large, whole, unpeeled fresh prawns or 500 g prawn tails, washed

2 tablespoons sea salt

1 tablespoon red wine vinegar

4 large sprigs of flat leaf parsley, leaves reserved and chopped (optional), stalks finely chopped

freshly squeezed juice of 2 lemons

2 tablespoons extra virgin olive oil

2 lemons, halved, to serve (optional)

serves 4

To devein the prawns, cut a slit down the back into the flesh and discard any black threads. Put 250 ml water in a saucepan, add the salt and bring to the boil. Add the prawns and stir in the vinegar and half the parsley stalks. Return to the boil, reduce the heat and cook gently for 2–4 minutes, stirring the prawns now and then, until their flesh turns dense, white and firm. The shells may change colour, often to pink or scarlet.

Remove the cooked prawns with a slotted spoon and transfer to a serving dish. Reserve 2 tablespoons of the cooking liquid and put in a small jug. Add the lemon juice, oil, remaining parsley stalks and parsley leaves, if using, and mix well. Pour this over the prawns. Let cool, then put in the refrigerator to marinate for 10-20 minutes.

Serve with the lemon halves, paper napkins, small bowls of water for cleaning fingers and containers for the discarded prawn shells.

trout fishcakes

Moist, with a lovely, earthy flavour, trout is perfect for making fishcakes. The cakes need to be chilled so they will keep their shape when fried.

Put the potatoes in a saucepan, cover with water and bring to the boil. Add the salt and simmer gently for 15 minutes until the potatoes are tender.

Meanwhile, put the fish in a large, shallow saucepan and pour over the milk. Cover, bring to the boil, reduce the heat and simmer gently for 5-6 minutes until the fish is opaque all the way through and just cooked. Using a slotted spoon, remove to a plate and let cool. Remove and discard the skin, then coarsely flake the fish.

Drain the potatoes and return them to the pan. Add the butter and mash until smooth. Put in a large bowl, add the parsley and chives and mix. Add plenty of salt and pepper. Using a large metal spoon, gently fold in the flaked fish.

Using floured hands, shape the mixture into 4 round cakes, about 2.5 cm thick. Dip them first into the beaten egg and then into the breadcrumbs to coat all over. Refrigerate for 30 minutes.

Put 2 cm oil in a frying pan and heat until hot. Add the fishcakes and fry over medium heat for 3-4 minutes on each side until golden and heated through.

To blanch the beans, bring a saucepan of water to the boil, add the beans and boil for 2-3 minutes until they turn bright green. Drain, run under cold water and drain again. Toss the beans and spinach in a bowl, divide between 4 plates and put a fishcake on top. Serve with extra chives and tartare sauce, if using.

500 g potatoes, peeled and cut into small chunks

½ teaspoon salt

500 g rainbow trout fillets

250 ml milk

25 g butter

a small bunch of flat leaf parsley, chopped

a small bunch of chives, chopped

flour, for shaping the fishcakes

1 egg, beaten

125 g fresh white breadcrumbs

sunflower oil, for frying

125 g fine green beans

125 g baby spinach leaves

sea salt and freshly ground black pepper

to serve

extra chives

tartare sauce (optional)

serves 4

bresaola and rocket
with olive oil and parmesan

This quick and simple starter, provides a truly delicious combination of flavours. Bresaola is Italian cured beef – flavourful, deep crimson, lean and succulent. Preferably it should be cut in very thin slices from the piece, but it is also available pre-sliced in packs. Serve it cool.

12–16 thin slices bresaola

50 g Parmesan cheese

1 large handful of wild rocket

4–6 teaspoons extra virgin olive oil

serves 4

Arrange the slices of bresaola on 4 serving plates.

Using a vegetable peeler or sharp knife, shave off thin curls of Parmesan and sprinkle them on top of the bresaola.

Add the wild rocket leaves, then drizzle with extra virgin olive oil and serve immediately.

peking-style duck pancake wraps

These hands-on starters always go down well. The paper wrappers will keep them moist and stop them sticking together if you want to prepare them in advance. Chinese Peking duck pancakes are sold in Chinese supermarkets in the freezer or chiller cabinet.

4 duck breasts, 150 g each
1 tablespoon salt
4 tablespoons dark soy sauce
1 tablespoon clear honey
2 teaspoons five-spice powder
1 tablespoon peanut oil

to serve

1 cucumber, about 30 cm long
24 Chinese Peking duck pancakes
125 ml hoisin sauce
6 spring onions, halved lengthways and crossways
sweet chilli sauce (optional)

24 squares of greaseproof paper, 12 x 12 cm

makes 24

Score the duck fat diagonally at 5-mm intervals and rub in the salt. Mix the soy sauce, honey and five-spice in a shallow dish. Put the duck breasts, skin side up, in the marinade, moving them about to coat the flesh. Put in the refrigerator to marinate for at least 2 hours.

Remove the duck from the marinade and pat dry with kitchen paper.

Heat the oil in a frying pan, add the duck breasts, skin side down, and cook for 8 minutes. Pour off the fat from the pan, then turn the breasts and cook the other side for 4 minutes. Let cool, then slice each duck breast diagonally into 6 strips.

Quarter the cucumber lengthways and scoop out and discard the seeds. Slice each quarter in 6 lengthways and then in half crossways. You should have 48 pieces.

Steam the pancakes for 5 minutes over boiling water. To assemble, work on 3–4 pancakes at a time and keep the others covered so they don't dry out. Spread 1 teaspoon hoisin sauce on each pancake, add a piece of duck, a few strips of cucumber and a piece of spring onion. Fold up the bottom, then the sides. Wrap the pieces of paper around the pockets in the same way. Cover with a cloth until ready to serve.

soups

celeriac, saffron and orange soup

2 tablespoons butter
or olive oil

1 large onion, chopped

1 celeriac, about 750 g, peeled
and cut into cubes (make up
the weight with potatoes,
if necessary)

1 litre vegetable stock

½ teaspoon saffron strands,
lightly ground in a mortar

1 tablespoon honey

grated zest and juice of
1 large unwaxed orange

sea salt and freshly ground
black pepper

crème fraîche or thick plain
yoghurt, to serve

parsley gremolata

(optional)

1 garlic clove

1 teaspoon coarse sea salt

a handful of fresh flat
leaf parsley

2 tablespoons olive oil

serves 4

This elegant, rich soup can be made dairy-free for any vegan guests by using olive oil instead of butter and leaving out the crème fraîche or yoghurt. Although the parsley gremolata is optional, it lifts both the colour and the flavour.

Heat the butter or oil in a saucepan, add the onion and cook until softened. Add the celeriac and potato, if using, cover and cook for 10 minutes, stirring occasionally. Add the stock, saffron, honey, orange zest and juice, salt and pepper. Bring to the boil, then simmer for 20 minutes until the vegetables are tender. Using a hand-held stick blender, purée until smooth. Alternatively, transfer to a blender or food processor and blend, in batches if necessary.

To make the gremolata, if using, put all the ingredients in a food processor or spice grinder and purée until smooth. Alternatively, use a mortar and pestle.

To serve, ladle the soup into warmed bowls and spoon over the gremolata, if using, and crème fraîche or yoghurt.

butternut squash soup
with allspice and pine nuts

This is a quintessentially American soup, popular in both north and south. The key is the light spicing and roasting of the butternut squash to bring out the best of its sweet flavour.

1 medium butternut squash, halved lengthways and deseeded

25 g unsalted butter

1 large leek, trimmed and chopped

1 bay leaf

a few black peppercorns, crushed

4–5 allspice berries, crushed

600 ml vegetable stock

60 g pine nuts, toasted in a dry frying pan

crusty bread, to serve

a non-stick baking sheet

serves 4

Put the butternut squash halves flesh side down onto the baking sheet. Roast in a preheated oven at 190°C (375°F) Gas 5 for 45 minutes or until tender. Remove from the oven and, using a spoon, scoop the flesh out of the skins and transfer to a bowl. Discard the skins.

Put the butter in a large saucepan and melt over medium to low heat. Add the leek, bay leaf, peppercorns and allspice and fry gently until the leek begins to soften. Add the butternut squash, stock and 1 litre water. Bring to the boil, reduce the heat and simmer for about 10 minutes or until the leeks are very soft.

Remove and discard the bay leaf and transfer the soup to a blender or food processor. Add the pine nuts and blend until smooth, working in batches if necessary. Return the soup to the saucepan and reheat. Serve hot with crusty bread.

shiitake and field mushroom soup
with madeira and thyme

This soup is simplicity itself. There may seem to be a lot of mushrooms in the recipe, but they will shrink when cooked, releasing their intense juices to create an aromatic broth.

25 g butter

1 medium onion, chopped

2 garlic cloves, chopped

250 g shiitake mushrooms, torn or chopped into big chunks

250 g open-capped mushrooms or portobello mushrooms, torn or chopped into big chunks

500 ml vegetable stock

150 ml Madeira wine or dry sherry

a bunch of fresh thyme, tied with string

sea salt and freshly ground black pepper

to serve

double cream

chopped parsley

serves 4

Melt the butter in a large saucepan, add the onion and cook over low heat until softened and translucent. Add the garlic, mushrooms, salt and pepper. Increase the heat, cover and cook, stirring occasionally, until the mushrooms have softened and their juices have been released, about 5 minutes.

Pour in the stock and Madeira or sherry and drop in the bunch of thyme. Bring to the boil, then cover and simmer for 15 minutes. Remove the thyme. Using a hand-held stick blender, coarsely purée the mixture. Alternatively, transfer to a blender or food processor and blend, in batches if necessary.

Return the soup to the pan and reheat. Ladle into warmed bowls, top with a swirl of cream, chopped parsley and lots of black pepper to serve.

mexican gazpacho

Ice-cold and enhanced with avocado, lime, cumin and chilli, this soup is refreshingly hard to beat on a hot summer's day. For a special occasion, freeze coriander leaves in ice cubes and use them to give your soup a decorative finish.

2 garlic cloves

1 teaspoon coarse sea salt

30 cm cucumber, coarsely chopped

1 yellow pepper, deseeded and coarsely chopped

2 celery stalks, coarsely chopped

4 ripe tomatoes, coarsely chopped

1 red onion, coarsely chopped

1 litre fresh tomato juice

2 teaspoons cumin seeds, pan-toasted

1 teaspoon mild chilli powder

1 ripe avocado, halved and stoned

freshly squeezed juice of 2 limes

freshly ground black pepper

coriander leaves set in ice cubes or chopped coriander, to serve

serves 6

Using a mortar and pestle, pound the garlic with the salt until puréed. Put the cucumber, pepper, celery, tomatoes and onion in a bowl, add the puréed garlic and mix well.

Transfer half of the mixture to a food processor and pulse until chopped but still slightly chunky. Pour into a bowl. Pour the remaining mixture into a blender or food processor and blend until smooth. Add this to the bowl. Mix in the tomato juice, cumin, chilli powder and pepper to taste.

Chill in the refrigerator for several hours or overnight until very cold. If short of time, put the soup in the freezer for 30 minutes to chill.

Cut the avocado into small cubes, toss in the lime juice until well coated, then stir into the gazpacho.

To serve, ladle the soup into chilled bowls, then add a few ice cubes or sprinkle with chopped coriander.

andalusian chickpea soup
with chorizo, paprika and saffron

2 tablespoons extra virgin olive oil

1 onion, chopped

3 thin celery stalks, chopped, with leaves reserved

1 large carrot, chopped

2 garlic cloves, chopped

250 g chorizo, skinned, halved, then cut into 1-cm slices

400 g canned chickpeas, drained

1.75 litres chicken stock

¼ teaspoon hot *pimentón*

125 g spinach, tough stalks removed and leaves coarsely chopped

¼ teaspoon saffron threads, bruised in a mortar

Manchego or Parmesan cheese, shaved, to serve (optional)

serves 4 as a main course lunch

This hearty soup is a meal in itself. The special flavour comes from two typically Spanish spices, *pimentón* (Spanish oak-smoked paprika, made from a variety of capsicum or pepper) and its home-grown luxury spice, saffron.

Heat the oil in a large saucepan and add the onion, celery and carrot. Gently sauté the vegetables until they begin to soften. Add the garlic, chorizo, chickpeas, stock and *pimentón*. Bring to the boil, reduce the heat and simmer for about 10 minutes. Add the spinach and celery leaves and simmer for 15 minutes.

Add the saffron and clean out the mortar using a little of the stock (so as not to waste any of the expensive saffron). Add to the saucepan and simmer for another 5 minutes.

Serve hot in warmed bowls as a main-course lunch. Add shavings of cheese, if using. This soup is very filling, but serve some good crusty bread and perhaps some extra cheese alongside if your guests are hungry.

spicy thai chicken soup

1.25 litres chicken stock

350 g boneless, skinless chicken breasts, thinly sliced

2 garlic cloves, chopped

2 stalks of lemongrass, halved lengthways

3 tablespoons fish sauce or light soy sauce

3 cm fresh ginger, peeled and grated

3 cm fresh galangal, peeled and sliced (optional)

8 small spring onions, quartered

50 g creamed coconut, chopped

4 fresh kaffir lime leaves, crushed (optional)

2 green bird's eye chillies, crushed

a large handful of fresh coriander leaves, torn

250 g uncooked tiger prawns, tails only, peeled or unpeeled*

freshly squeezed juice of 2 limes

serves 4

*Do not use cooked prawns as the texture will be disappointing. If you prefer, you could use cubes of other fresh fish instead.

This is a really tasty soup. Lemongrass and kaffir lime leaves are sold in supermarkets as part of the packs of fresh Thai herbs and flavourings that are now available. You could use lemon and lime zest instead if you can't find them, but avoid dried Thai spices from the spice rack – they're just not intense and aromatic enough.

Put the stock in a large saucepan and bring to the boil. Add the chicken, garlic, lemongrass, fish sauce or soy sauce, ginger, spring onions and creamed coconut.

Return to the boil, part-cover, reduce the heat to a high simmer and cook for 5 minutes. Add the kaffir lime leaves, if using, the chillies, half the coriander leaves and the prawns.

Simmer gently for 5 minutes or until the chicken is cooked through and the prawn flesh is densely white. Do not overcook or the prawns will be tough. Add the lime juice and serve in warmed soup bowls, topped with the remaining coriander leaves.

Note: Remove the chillies before drinking the soup. They are fiery, but leaving them whole and merely crushing them releases a gentle, not violent, heat.

salads

A green salad is the easiest of dishes to assemble, but, to be successful, the ingredients must be of very good quality. Choose a selection of leaves (soft and crisp, sweet and bitter), then dress with best extra virgin olive oil, the lightest touch of lemon juice or vinegar and just the right amount of seasoning.

fresh green salad

2 handfuls of peppery leaves, such as rocket or watercress

2 handfuls of bitter leaves, such as frisée

2 handfuls of crisp green lettuce, such as Little Gem or cos, torn

1 small head of chicory, separated into leaves

1 small handful of baby spinach leaves

leaves from a small bunch of flat leaf parsley, dill or mint (optional)

1 small onion, thinly sliced into rings

dressing

2 garlic cloves, crushed

½ teaspoon sea salt flakes

1–1½ tablespoons freshly squeezed lemon juice

4–6 tablespoons extra virgin olive oil

serves 4

To make the dressing, put the garlic, salt and half the lemon juice in a small bowl and mix with a hand-held stick blender or a fork. Slowly pour in the oil and blend or mix until emulsified. Taste, then add enough lemon juice to give bite. Alternatively, use a mortar and pestle to crush the garlic and salt, then proceed.

Put the washed leaves, herbs, if using, and onion rings in a large bowl, cover with a plastic bag, seal and chill until ready to serve, so the leaves stay crisp and fresh.

Just before serving, trickle the dressing over the leaves and toss thoroughly with your hands or wooden spoons.

chicory and radicchio salad
with walnut dressing

The secret of this salad is to have the walnuts sizzling hot. Get the salad ready and add the walnuts as soon as they come out of the oven. Walnut oil is great in dressings, but just use extra olive oil if you can't find it. Keep nuts and nut oils (except peanut oil) in the refrigerator, because they can go rancid quickly.

100 g walnuts

1 teaspoon walnut oil

1 teaspoon sea salt

1 head of radicchio, leaves separated, washed and dried

2 heads of chicory, leaves separated, washed and dried

1 small curly endive lettuce, leaves separated, washed and dried

walnut dressing

1 tablespoon walnut oil

1 tablespoon extra virgin olive oil

a good squeeze of fresh lemon juice

freshly ground black pepper

a baking sheet

serves 4

Put the walnuts, walnut oil and salt in a small bowl and stir. Transfer to a baking sheet in a single layer and cook in a preheated oven at 200°C (400°F) Gas 6 for 8–10 minutes until toasted all over.

Meanwhile, put the salad leaves in a large salad bowl. Put the oils and lemon juice in a separate bowl and whisk well. Add freshly ground black pepper to taste.

To serve, sprinkle the hot walnuts over the salad leaves, pour over the dressing and toss well. Serve immediately as a salad or with crusty bread and shavings of Parmesan as a lunch or salad starter.

mozzarella, tomato and basil salad

Insalata Caprese is a favourite Italian salad, sporting the colours of the national flag and just the simplest of dressings. There is nothing better than a little ground sea salt and pepper, and the traditional healthy sprinkling of the best extra virgin olive oil.

500 g mozzarella cheese, preferably buffalo, sliced or torn

8 ripe Italian plum tomatoes, such as Martino, Perini or San Marzano, thickly sliced

a large handful of basil leaves

extra virgin olive oil, for sprinkling

sea salt and freshly ground black pepper

Italian bread, such as ciabatta, to serve

serves 4

Put about 3 slices or chunks of mozzarella on each plate. Add 3 slices of tomato, sprinkle with salt and pepper, then top with basil (basil should be torn, not cut, for the best flavour and appearance).

Alternatively, arrange the tomato and mozzarella slices in lines on a large serving platter, then add salt, pepper and basil leaves as before.

Sprinkle olive oil generously over the salad and serve with plenty of Italian bread.

vegetarian caesar salad

This classic salad never seems to lose its appeal and is constantly being updated. The original recipe calls for barely cooked eggs, but boiled eggs cooked until the yolks are just set make a fantastic dressing. For this vegetarian alternative, anchovies have been replaced with vegetarian Worcestershire sauce.

1 cos lettuce, outer leaves removed, or 2 small lettuce hearts

freshly grated Parmesan cheese, to serve

croutons

2 thick slices white bread, cubed

1 tablespoon olive oil

dressing

2 eggs

4 tablespoons freshly grated Parmesan cheese

3 tablespoons white wine vinegar

2 teaspoons vegetarian Worcestershire sauce

1 tablespoon snipped chives (optional)

4 tablespoons olive oil

sea salt and freshly ground black pepper

a baking sheet

serves 4–6

To make the croutons, put the cubes of bread in a bowl, drizzle with the olive oil and toss until evenly coated. Tip onto a baking sheet and bake in a preheated oven at 190°C (375°F) Gas 5 until golden and crisp on all sides, about 10 minutes. Check the bread occasionally while cooking to see it doesn't burn. Let cool.

To make the dressing, put the eggs in a saucepan of cold water and bring to the boil. Cook for 5–6 minutes, then drain immediately and cool under cold running water. Peel the eggs when cold, then put in a small bowl and mash with a fork. Add the remaining dressing ingredients, except the oil, and whisk thoroughly. Gradually add the oil – a little at a time – whisking until emulsified.

Tear the lettuce into pieces and put in a large bowl, pour over the dressing and toss until well coated. Top with the croutons, sprinkle with Parmesan and serve.

warm chickpea salad
with spiced mushrooms

This main-course salad is inspired by Middle Eastern cuisine, where beans, yoghurt and mint are widely used. Make this dish more substantial by serving it on a bed of couscous or bulghur wheat.

3 tablespoons olive oil

300 g button mushrooms

2 garlic cloves, chopped

1 red chilli, deseeded and chopped

400 g canned chickpeas, rinsed and drained

2 teaspoons ground cumin

freshly squeezed juice of 1 lemon

175 ml Greek or thick plain yoghurt

a large handful of mint leaves, chopped

250 g baby spinach leaves

sea salt and freshly ground black pepper

serves 4

Heat 2 tablespoons of the oil a frying pan. Add the mushrooms, season with salt and cook until softened. Reduce the heat, then add the garlic, chilli and chickpeas. Fry for 2 minutes, then add the cumin and half the lemon juice. Cook until the juices in the pan evaporate, then remove from the heat and set aside.

Put the yoghurt in a bowl, then add the chopped mint and the remaining lemon juice and oil. Add salt and pepper and mix until blended.

Divide the spinach between 4 plates or put on a serving platter, add the chickpea and mushroom mixture, then pour the yoghurt dressing over the top and serve.

lobster and fennel salad

This simple salad is packed with flavour. When you serve lobster, the effect is instant 'special occasion'. Who would ever guess the dish was so simple to prepare? Make the mayonnaise if you have the time, the result will be superior to any shop-bought alternative.

1 large bulb of fennel

freshly squeezed juice of ½ lemon

4 tablespoons extra virgin olive oil

4 small cooked lobsters, about 500 g each, or 2 large ones

sea salt and freshly ground black pepper

mayonnaise

2 egg yolks

2 teaspoons white wine vinegar or freshly squeezed lemon juice

¼ teaspoon salt

2 teaspoons Dijon mustard

300 ml extra virgin olive oil

serves 4

To make the mayonnaise, put the egg yolks, vinegar or lemon juice, salt and mustard in a food processor and blend until frothy. With the machine running, slowly pour in the oil until the sauce is thick and glossy. You may have to thin it slightly by blending in 1–2 tablespoons boiling water. Season to taste with pepper. Cover the surface with clingfilm and store in the refrigerator for up to 5 days.

Trim off and discard the tough outer layer of fennel, then chop and reserve the fronds. Cut the bulb in half, then crossways into very thin slices. Put in a bowl, add the lemon juice, oil, fennel fronds, salt and pepper, toss well, then marinate for 15 minutes.

Cut the lobsters in half and lift the tail flesh out of the shell. Crack the claws with a small hammer or crab crackers and carefully remove all the meat.

Put a layer of shaved fennel salad on each plate, top with the lobster and serve with a spoonful of mayonnaise.

seared tuna salad
with lime and soy dressing

The availability of quality fresh tuna has made it one of today's most popular fish. It is a joy to cook and eat.

300 g fresh tuna steak

3 heads of chicory, leaves separated

2 bunches of watercress

dressing

grated zest and freshly squeezed juice of 2 unwaxed limes, plus extra wedges, to serve

1 chilli, finely chopped

100 ml light soy sauce

2 kaffir lime leaves, thinly sliced

1 stalk of lemongrass, very thinly sliced

3 tablespoons olive oil

sea salt and freshly ground black pepper

serves 8

Heat a stove-top grill pan until very hot, then add the tuna steak. Cook for 2–3 minutes on each side. Don't move it around before this or it will not have formed a good crust and will break up. Remove to a carving board and let rest.

To make the dressing, put the lime zest and juice in a bowl. Add the chilli, soy sauce, kaffir lime leaves, lemongrass, oil and salt and pepper to taste. Arrange the chicory on serving plates.

Cut the tuna crossways into thin slices and arrange on top of the salad. Add the watercress and wedges of lime, spoon the dressing over the top and serve.

roasted aubergine and parma ham salad

Grilled Parma ham is far better than crispy bacon, so start cooking and impress with this simple but delicious salad.

200 g cherry tomatoes

2 small aubergines, sliced lengthways

2 tablespoons olive oil

4 slices Parma ham

a bunch of rocket

sea salt and freshly ground black pepper

dressing

1 tablespoon balsamic vinegar

1 tablespoon Dijon mustard

3 tablespoons extra virgin olive oil

serves 4

Slice off and discard the top of each tomato, then put them, cut side up, in an oiled roasting tin. Add the aubergines. Sprinkle with the olive oil, salt and pepper. Cook in a preheated oven at 180°C (350°F) Gas 4 for 15 minutes, then reduce to 150°C (300°F) Gas 2 and cook for a further 15 minutes, until the tomatoes have burst their skins. Remove from the oven and set aside.

Cook the Parma ham under a hot grill for about 3 minutes on each side, until crisp.

To make the dressing, put the vinegar and mustard in a small bowl and mix until smooth. Gradually add the oil, mixing well, then add salt and pepper to taste.

Arrange the rocket and roasted aubergines and tomatoes on 4 plates and spoon over the dressing. Top with the Parma ham and serve warm or at room temperature.

chicken liver salad

This salad makes a wonderful starter or supper dish. Be careful not to overcook the chicken livers, otherwise they will become dry and tough, instead of juicy and soft. Chicken livers are available in butcher's shops and large supermarkets, fresh or frozen.

4 slices toasted or fried bread

200 g mixed lettuce leaves

200 g chicken livers

50 g butter

2 tablespoons olive oil

100 ml red wine

sea salt and freshly ground black pepper

serves 4

Put the toast on 4 small salad plates and top with the mixed lettuce leaves.

Trim the chicken livers, removing any tubes, membranes and any dark or slightly green patches. Cut the livers into equal bite-sized pieces.

Melt the butter and olive oil in a large saucepan. When really hot, add the chicken livers and cook for 2 minutes on one side, then turn them over and cook for 2 minutes more.

Add salt and pepper, then carefully remove the livers from the saucepan, using a slotted spoon, and divide them between the plates, laying them on top of the lettuce leaves.

Add the wine to the pan juices and bring to the boil, stirring. Boil hard for 1 minute, then pour the hot dressing over the livers and serve immediately.

warm chicken and chorizo salad

3 mild or spicy chorizo sausages, about 100 g, cut crossways into coin-shaped slices, or a 150 g piece, cut into chunks

12–16 baby courgettes, about 300 g, halved lengthways

500 g boneless, skinless, cooked or smoked chicken, shredded into strips

250 g mixed red and green lettuce leaves

1 bag rocket or watercress, about 100 g

16–20 dry-cured black olives, about 75 g

sprigs of coriander or flat leaf parsley

garlic bread, toasted ciabatta or warmed focaccia, to serve

vinaigrette

2 tablespoons balsamic vinegar

6 tablespoons extra virgin olive oil

2 garlic cloves, crushed

sea salt and freshly ground black pepper

serves 4

Chorizo – Spanish salami – adds extra pizzazz to many dishes. Fry it first to release all the smoky paprika juices. Nothing could be simpler or have more impact. It's available from supermarkets, good delicatessens and Hispanic grocers.

Heat a non-stick frying pan or stove-top grill pan, add the chorizo slices or chunks, then fry gently on all sides until the juices run and the edges are slightly crisp. Set aside.

Put the vinaigrette ingredients in a small bowl or jug and mix well. Use some of the mixture to brush the courgette halves, then add them to the still-hot pan and cook for 5 minutes on each side or until hot and golden.

Put the chicken in a large salad bowl and add the lettuce leaves, rocket or watercress and olives. Sprinkle with the remaining vinaigrette, then add the courgette, the chorizo and its juices and the coriander or parsley. Toss well, then serve immediately with your choice of bread.

seared peppered beef salad

A summery way of enjoying roast beef without too much heat from the kitchen. Par-boiling the potatoes before roasting means that they won't dry out and shrivel as they roast.

500 g baby new potatoes, unpeeled

2 tablespoons olive oil

250 g baby plum tomatoes

4 fillet steaks, 125 g each

1 tablespoon Worcestershire sauce

100 g wild rocket

125 g sugar snap peas, trimmed, blanched, refreshed and halved lengthways

sea salt and freshly ground black pepper

horseradish dressing

3 tablespoons crème fraîche

1–2 tablespoons creamed horseradish

a squeeze of fresh lemon juice

serves 4

Bring a large saucepan of water to the boil, add the potatoes and par-boil for 12–15 minutes until nearly cooked through. Drain and transfer to a roasting tin. Drizzle with 1 tablespoon oil and toss to coat. Sprinkle with salt and pepper and roast in a preheated oven at 220°C (425°F) Gas 7 for 25–30 minutes until browned and starting to crisp.

Remove from the oven and, using a large metal spoon, push the potatoes to one end of the tin in a pile. Put the baby plum tomatoes in the empty half of the tin and sprinkle with 1 tablespoon olive oil, salt and pepper. Roast in the oven for 15 minutes until just soft.

Meanwhile, put all the horseradish dressing ingredients in a bowl and mix. Add salt and pepper to taste. Set aside. Sprinkle the steaks with plenty of black pepper and drizzle with the Worcestershire sauce. Preheat a stove-top grill pan, add the steak and sear for 1–2 minutes on each side or until cooked to your liking. Set aside to rest.

Put the rocket and sugar snap peas in a bowl and toss. Divide between 4 plates. Spoon the potatoes and tomatoes around the rocket and peas.

Slice the steak diagonally and arrange the slices over the salad. Top with a dollop of horseradish dressing and serve, with any remaining sauce in a separate bowl.

vegetables & vegetarian mains

baked aubergine and tomato stacks

1 aubergine, about 250 g, sliced into 12 thick rounds

1 large beefsteak tomato, about 150 g, sliced into 8 rounds

250 g Taleggio cheese, or any other good melting cheese, cut into 12 slices

extra virgin olive oil, for brushing and sprinkling

a ceramic baking dish, oiled

serves 4

This is a filling vegetarian dish, topped with bubbly, browned cheese. Taleggio – which is full of nuttiness when melted – is used here, but try any other good melting cheese, such as Fontina, Gruyère or mozzarella. Beefsteak tomatoes are perfect for this dish because they are delightfully large and easy to slice and stack well.

Lightly brush a frying pan with the oil and heat until hot. Working in batches, add the aubergine slices and cook for a few minutes on each side until browned and slightly soft.

To make the stacks, place 4 slices of aubergine apart in the baking dish. Put 1 slice of tomato on top of each one, then 1 slice of cheese. Repeat until each stack has 3 slices of aubergine, 2 of tomato and 3 of cheese, ending with a cheese slice on top. Sprinkle each stack with olive oil.

Bake in a preheated oven at 190°C (375°F) Gas 5 for about 15 minutes until soft, bubbly and golden. Serve hot.

provençal tian

A *tian* is a shallow clay dish in the language of Provence and also anything cooked in it. Vegetables such as tomatoes and courgettes are prone to lose a lot of liquid, so it's a good idea to remove some beforehand by roasting or salting (this is known as 'degorging').

6 large ripe tomatoes, halved

4 garlic cloves, thinly sliced

6 small aubergines, thickly sliced lengthways

3 green or yellow courgettes, thickly sliced lengthways

6 tablespoons olive oil, plus extra for brushing

2 large red onions, thickly sliced

2 tablespoons chopped fresh thyme leaves

sea salt and freshly ground black pepper

sprigs of basil, to serve (optional)

topping

grated zest of 1 unwaxed lemon

3 garlic cloves, crushed

about 140 g dried breadcrumbs

6 tablespoons freshly grated Parmesan cheese

a baking sheet

a tian or other shallow ceramic ovenproof dish

serves 4–6

Put the tomatoes on a baking sheet, cut side up, and push slivers of garlic into each one. Roast in a preheated oven at 200°C (400°F) Gas 6 for about 30 minutes to remove some of the moisture.

Meanwhile, put the aubergines and courgettes on a plate, sprinkle with salt and set aside for 30 minutes to extract some of the moisture. Rinse and pat dry with kitchen paper.

Heat the oil in a large frying pan, add the onion and sauté until softened and translucent. Remove from the pan and spread over the base of a *tian* or other shallow ceramic ovenproof dish.

Arrange overlapping layers of the tomatoes, aubergines and courgettes on top – place them in lines across the dish, like fish scales. Tuck the thyme between the layers and season with pepper. Brush with the extra olive oil and cook in a preheated oven at 200°C (400°F) Gas 6 for 20 minutes.

Meanwhile, to make the topping, put the lemon zest and the crushed garlic in a bowl and mix well. Stir in the breadcrumbs and cheese, then sprinkle over the top of the *tian*. Continue cooking for at least 30 minutes or until browned, finishing under the grill if necessary. Serve topped with basil leaves, if using.

The colours in this casserole are equalled only by its flavour. Both are startling and gorgeous. Don't overdo the harissa – a little is enough to wake you up! Let the vegetables caramelize and acquire a barbecue flavour.

north african charred vegetables

3 red onions, cut into wedges

18 cherry tomatoes

1 large courgette, cut into wedges

150 g small red potatoes, halved

2 red peppers, deseeded and cut into strips or wedges

1 yellow pepper, deseeded and cut into strips or wedges

2 fennel bulbs, cut into wedges

6 tablespoons olive oil

6 garlic cloves, crushed to a paste

½ teaspoon harissa paste

1 teaspoon ground cumin

1 tablespoon vinegar

1 tablespoon chopped fresh mint

1 tablespoon chopped fresh coriander

2 teaspoons sea salt

500 ml Greek yoghurt, to serve

a shallow casserole dish

serves 4–6

Reserve 1 onion and 4 cherry tomatoes. Arrange the remaining vegetables in a roasting tin, drizzle with 4 tablespoons of the oil and roast in a preheated oven at 240°C (475°F) Gas 9 or the highest temperature available until they begin to char, about 30 minutes.

Lower the heat to 180°C (350°F) Gas 4. Remove the vegetables from the oven and transfer to a shallow casserole dish.

Put the crushed garlic in a small bowl and mash in the harissa, cumin and remaining oil. Stir in the vinegar, mint and coriander. Mix this in with the vegetables, tuck in the last onion and 4 cherry tomatoes, sprinkle generously with salt and return the casserole to the oven to bake for a further 25 minutes.

If there is too much liquid, pour it off into a small saucepan, bring to the boil and simmer until reduced and concentrated in flavour. Pour back into the casserole.

Serve with lashings of yoghurt.

chickpea and tomato masala
with beans and coriander

1 thick slice fresh ginger, chopped

2 garlic cloves, coarsely chopped

2 tablespoons sunflower oil

¼ teaspoon ground turmeric

3 fresh green chillies, halved

1 teaspoon cumin seeds

1 onion, halved lengthways,
then sliced into half-rings

250 g green beans

800 g canned chickpeas,
rinsed and drained

a pinch of ground cloves

a pinch of ground cinnamon

1 teaspoon ground coriander

¼ teaspoon ground cumin

250 g cherry tomatoes, quartered

sea salt and freshly ground black pepper

to serve

chopped coriander leaves (optional)

Indian bread, such as pooris, chapattis or
naan bread, or buttered pita breads

serves 4–6

A satisfying dish with Indian flavours in which, instead of a smooth tomato-based sauce, cherry tomatoes are folded in at the last moment. It is based on *chole* or *channa masala*, a great vegetarian dish found all over India.

Using a mortar and pestle, mash the ginger and garlic to a chunky paste. Heat the oil in a saucepan, add the turmeric, chillies and cumin seeds and fry briefly. Add the onions and fry for about 6 minutes. Add the ginger and garlic paste and fry for a further 2–3 minutes until the onions have softened.

Add the green beans and 150 ml water, then bring to the boil. Lower the heat and cook gently for 10 minutes. Add the chickpeas, ground cloves, cinnamon, coriander and cumin. Add salt and pepper to taste and mix well. Cook for a further 9 minutes. Gently fold in the cherry tomatoes with a wooden spoon. Turn off the heat, cover and steam for 1–2 minutes. Sprinkle with chopped coriander, if using, and serve with your choice of bread.

pumpkin and tofu laksa

Laksa is a Malaysian curry with rice noodles, crunchy raw vegetables and fragrant herbs bathed in a spicy coconut soup. If you can't find lemongrass or kaffir lime leaves, replace them with lime zest and lemon juice.

250 g peeled, deseeded pumpkin or butternut squash, cut into 1 cm cubes

sunflower oil, for frying

300 g tofu, dried with kitchen paper and cut into 4 triangles

200 g creamed coconut, chopped and dissolved in 500 ml boiling water, or 800 ml coconut milk

4 tablespoons light soy sauce

2 teaspoons sugar

150 g rice vermicelli noodles

150 g beansprouts

1 medium tomato, cut into 8 wedges

5 cm cucumber, cut into thin strips

8 sprigs of coriander

a large handful of mint leaves

2 spring onions, chopped

sea salt

spice paste

2 garlic cloves, coarsely chopped

2 red chillies, deseeded and coarsely chopped

5 cm fresh ginger, peeled and finely grated

1 small onion

¼ teaspoon ground turmeric

2 stalks of lemongrass, sliced

4 kaffir lime leaves, chopped

serves 4

To make the spice paste, put all the ingredients and 3 tablespoons water in a blender or spice grinder and purée until smooth (add more water if necessary).

Put the pumpkin or squash in a saucepan, then add salt and 500 ml water. Bring to the boil, then simmer for 10 minutes until the cubes are tender but still chunky. Drain, reserving the cooking liquid.

Heat 2 cm sunflower oil in a wok or frying pan. Add the tofu and fry until golden and crisp all over. Carefully remove with a slotted spoon and drain on crumpled kitchen paper. Set aside.

Heat 2 tablespoons of the oil in a saucepan, add the spice paste and fry for 2 minutes to release the aromas. Add the coconut liquid or coconut milk, fried tofu, soy sauce and sugar. Add the reserved pumpkin liquid. Bring to the boil, then simmer for 10 minutes.

Meanwhile, put the noodles in a bowl, cover with boiling water and let soak for 5 minutes. Drain and divide between 4 warmed bowls.

Add the beansprouts, tomato and cooked pumpkin or squash. Place a piece of fried tofu in each bowl. Ladle over the hot coconut soup, top with the cucumber, coriander, mint and spring onions, then serve.

roasted teriyaki tofu steaks

Dark soy sauce, sweet mirin and dry sake give teriyaki its
unique flavours. You can buy it ready-made, but this only
faintly resembles the real thing, so make your own – it's easy.

500 g fresh firm tofu, cut into 4 pieces

4 fresh or dried shiitake mushrooms (optional)

200 g fresh or dried egg noodles

teriyaki marinade

125 ml dark soy sauce

125 ml mirin (Japanese sweet rice wine)

125 ml sake

1 tablespoon sugar

glazed green vegetables

2 tablespoons sunflower oil

2 garlic cloves, thinly sliced

200 g young purple sprouting broccoli or
broccoli florets, chopped

1 leek, white and light green parts, thinly sliced

200 g bok choy, quartered lengthways

1 fennel bulb, trimmed and thinly sliced

2 teaspoons cornflour mixed with
4 tablespoons cold water

to serve

2 spring onions, thinly sliced diagonally

1 tablespoon sesame seeds, pan-toasted

a baking dish, lightly oiled

serves 4

To make the marinade, put the soy sauce, mirin, sake and sugar
in a large frying pan and heat, stirring until the sugar has dissolved.
Add the tofu and mushrooms, if using. Simmer gently for about
15 minutes, turning the tofu over halfway through cooking.

Transfer the tofu steaks to a lightly oiled baking dish or roasting tin.
Spoon a little sauce on top and roast in a preheated oven at 220°C
(425°F) Gas 7 for 10 minutes. Keep them warm in a low oven.
Using a slotted spoon, remove the mushrooms from the remaining
sauce, squeeze dry and slice thinly. Reserve the sauce.

To make the glazed vegetables, heat a wok until hot, then add the
oil. Add the garlic, broccoli, leek and sliced mushrooms and stir-fry
for 2 minutes. Add the bok choy and fennel. Stir-fry for 2 minutes.
Add the reserved sauce and 75 ml water, stir, cover and cook for
2 minutes. Push the vegetables to the back of the wok, add the
cornflour mixture to the bubbling juices and stir until thickened. Mix
the vegetables into the sauce. Cook the noodles according to the
packet instructions, then drain.

To serve, put a nest of noodles on warmed plates and pile on the
vegetables. Top with the tofu steaks, then sprinkle with spring onions
and toasted sesame seeds.

green thai vegetable curry

This popular Thai classic is super-quick to make and always go down a storm.

3 tablespoons green Thai curry paste

400 ml canned coconut milk

425 ml vegetable stock

1 large potato, cut into 2.5 cm pieces

250 g broccoli florets

250 g cauliflower florets

125 g frozen petit pois

125 g sugar snap peas, halved lengthways

to serve

1 lime, cut into wedges

375 g Thai fragrant rice

serves 4

To cook the Thai fragrant rice, rinse to remove the starch, put in a large saucepan and add cold water to 2.5 cm above the rice level. Cover with a lid and bring to the boil, reduce the heat and simmer until the water is absorbed, about 5 minutes. Remove the pan from the heat and let stand, with the lid on, for about 10 minutes until cooked.

Meanwhile, put the curry paste in a wok, heat and cook for 2 minutes, stirring. Add the coconut milk, stock and potato. Bring to the boil, reduce the heat and simmer for 5 minutes. Add the broccoli and cauliflower florets, stalk end down, cover with a lid and simmer for 4 minutes. Add the peas and cook for a further 2 minutes until all the vegetables are tender.

Ladle the curry into 4 warmed bowls and serve with lime wedges and the Thai fragrant rice.

roquefort tart
with walnut and toasted garlic dressing

Roquefort is a salty French blue cheese that's made with ewes' milk. You could substitute any good-quality blue cheese when making this recipe.

1 recipe Pâte Brisée (page 235)

225 g cream cheese or curd cheese (such as Philadelphia)

150 ml crème fraîche or double cream

3 medium eggs, beaten

175 g Roquefort

freshly grated nutmeg, to taste

3 tablespoons chopped fresh chives

freshly ground black pepper

walnut and toasted garlic dressing

3 garlic cloves, very thinly sliced

2 tablespoons olive oil

75 g walnut halves

1 tablespoon walnut oil

3 tablespoons chopped fresh parsley

a loose-based tart tin, 25 cm diameter

foil or baking parchment and baking beans

serves 6

Bring the pastry to room temperature. Roll out the pastry thinly on a lightly floured work surface, then use to line the tart tin. Prick the base, then chill or freeze for 15 minutes. Line the base with foil or baking parchment, then fill with baking beans. Set on a baking sheet and bake 'blind' in the centre of a preheated oven at 200°C (400°F) Gas 6 for 10–12 minutes. Remove the foil or baking parchment and baking beans and return the pastry case to the oven for a further 5–7 minutes.

To make the filling, put the cream cheese or curd cheese in a bowl and beat until softened. Beat in the crème fraîche or cream and the eggs. Crumble in the Roquefort and mix gently. Season with lots of black pepper and nutmeg. Stir in the chives and set aside.

Let the pastry case cool slightly and lower the oven to 190°C (375°F) Gas 5. Pour the filling into the case and bake for 30–35 minutes or until the filling is puffed and golden brown.

Meanwhile, to make the walnut and garlic dressing, heat the olive oil in a frying pan and add the garlic and walnuts. Stir-fry until the garlic is golden and the walnuts browned. Stir in the walnut oil and parsley.

Serve the tart warm or at room temperature with the warm dressing.

minted char-grilled courgettes

4 medium courgettes, about 1 kg

2 tablespoons olive oil

4 teaspoons white wine vinegar

a handful of mint, leaves torn

sea salt and freshly ground black pepper

serves 4

Perfect for a summer lunch, this Mediterranean recipe and simple char-grilling technique bring out the best in courgettes. They cook to a sensuous texture and absorb the contrasting flavours of the tangy vinegar and fragrant mint.

Trim off and discard the ends of the courgettes, then cut the courgettes lengthways into ribbon-like slices and put in a bowl. Drizzle with the olive oil and, using your hands, gently toss the slices until well coated.

Heat a stove-top grill pan or non-stick frying pan until very hot. Add the courgette ribbons (in batches if necessary) and cook until softened and marked with black stripes on both sides. Transfer to a shallow dish and drizzle with the vinegar while they are still warm. Add salt and pepper and let cool.

To serve, pile the courgette ribbons in a serving bowl and sprinkle with the mint leaves.

chilli greens with garlic crisps

'Greens' – used loosely to describe any leafy green vegetable – include spring greens, Swiss chard, bok choy, beetroot leaves, spinach and more. Many need only brief cooking – steaming or stir-frying to retain their colour, nutrients and flavour. Remove any tough stalks before you start.

500 g greens (see introduction right)

2 tablespoons olive oil

4 garlic cloves, sliced

1 red chilli, deseeded and thinly sliced

sea salt and freshly ground black pepper

serves 4

Coarsely chop the greens, but, if using bok choy, cut lengthways into wedges. Gently heat the olive oil in a large saucepan. Add the garlic, fry until golden and crisp, about 2–3 minutes, then remove and set aside. Add the chilli to the infused oil in the pan and cook for 1 minute.

Tip in the greens – they will splutter, so stand back. Add salt and pepper and mix well. Cover and cook, turning occasionally using tongs, until tender: spring greens, about 5 minutes; Swiss chard, bok choy and beetroot leaves, about 3 minutes; and spinach, about 1–2 minutes.

Transfer to a warmed serving dish and top with the garlic crisps.

This easy, delicious dish can be used in lots of ways – piled on top of a pizza base, as an accompaniment to a main course or as a starter .

catalan spinach

with garlic, pine nuts and raisins

2 tablespoons extra virgin olive oil, preferably Spanish

3 tablespoons pine nuts

2 garlic cloves, crushed

6 canned anchovy fillets, chopped

500 g well-washed spinach, water still clinging

3 tablespoons seedless raisins

sea salt and cracked black pepper, to serve

serves 4

Heat the oil in a non-stick frying pan. Carefully add the pine nuts, stir-fry for about 1 minute until golden, then remove quickly with a slotted spoon or drain through a sieve, reserving the oil and returning it to the pan.

Add the garlic and anchovies to the pan and mash them together over a medium heat until aromatic, then add the wet spinach and raisins. Toss carefully with non-stick tongs or wooden spoons until evenly distributed. Cover the pan and cook over medium heat for 2–3 minutes, stirring halfway through.

Uncover the pan, sprinkle with the pine nuts and toss well until gleaming. Serve hot or warm, with small dishes of salt and cracked black pepper.

provençal roasted vegetables

Preparation is kept to a minimum and the result is a thing of beauty. Make sure you provide a side plate to put the bits on as people pluck their way through the sweet, juicy vegetables.

1 aubergine

2 courgettes

4 red onions, unpeeled

2 red chillies

1 whole head of garlic, unpeeled

4 tomatoes on the vine or 16 cherry tomatoes on the vine

4 sprigs of rosemary

10 tablespoons olive oil

freshly squeezed juice of ½ lemon

coarse sea salt and freshly ground black pepper

serves 4

Cut the aubergine lengthways into quarters and score the flesh with a criss-cross pattern. Slice the courgettes in half lengthways. Cut a thin slice off the bottom of the onions and cut a cross in the top. Split the chillies in half. Leave the garlic whole.

Put all the vegetables, except the tomatoes, cut side up in a roasting tin or dish. Tuck the rosemary and chillies into the onions. Brush all but 2 tablespoons of oil all over the vegetables, then drizzle with the lemon juice and add salt and pepper.

Roast in a preheated oven at 200°C (400°F) Gas 6 for 30 minutes, then brush the tomatoes with the remaining oil and put on top of the half-roasted vegetables. Cook for 15–20 minutes until the vegetables are golden and the tomatoes have split. If using cherry tomatoes, add them after 40 minutes and roast for a further 5–10 minutes. Serve.

lemon-roasted baby potatoes

Potatoes love to be roasted. These zesty little spuds have a crisp, tangy exterior and are fluffy inside. Serve with steamed greens or roasted vegetables.

1 kg baby new potatoes, scrubbed

4 tablespoons olive oil

2 unwaxed lemons, grated zest of both and juice of 1

1 teaspoon sugar

sea salt and freshly ground black pepper

serves 4

Cook the potatoes in salted boiling water for 5 minutes, drain, then transfer to a roasting tin.

Put the olive oil, lemon zest and juice, sugar, salt and pepper in a bowl and whisk. Pour over the potatoes and toss well to coat.

Roast in a preheated oven at 190°C (375°F) Gas 5 for 20–30 minutes, turning and basting frequently with the pan juices, until golden and tender.

The ultimate comfort food, creamy mashed potatoes make the perfect partner for good-quality grilled sausages (page 163) or any other grilled meat. Choose large 'old' potatoes – the sort that become fluffy when mashed. When boiling potatoes, it's always important to add salt before cooking.

classic creamy mashed potatoes

1 kg large 'old' potatoes, such as baking potatoes, peeled and cut into 5 cm cubes

about 150 ml milk, preferably hot

40 g butter

sea salt and freshly ground black pepper

serves 4

Put the potatoes in a large saucepan. Add cold water to cover and a pinch of salt. Bring to the boil, reduce the heat, cover with a lid and simmer for 15–20 minutes until tender when pierced with a knife. Drain and return the potatoes to the pan.

Return the saucepan to the heat and mash the potatoes with a fork or potato masher for 30 seconds – this will steam off any excess water. Stir in the milk and butter with a spoon. Mash until smooth, adding extra milk if needed and salt and pepper to taste. Serve immediately in a serving bowl or straight onto dinner plates.

fish & seafood

steamed mussels
with garlic and vermouth in a foil parcel

The vermouth turns to steam in these parcels of foil and cooks the mussels in a delicious scented vapour. Let guests open their own parcels – as they do so they will breathe in the heavenly aroma.

1 kg mussels in their shells
50 g butter
150 ml dry vermouth
2 garlic cloves, crushed

to serve

crusty bread
a bunch of flat leaf parsley, coarsely chopped
(optional)

4 pieces of foil, about 60 x 30 cm
a baking sheet

serves 4

Scrub the mussels clean and rinse them in several changes of cold water to remove grit. Pull off the beards or seaweed-like threads and discard any mussels that are cracked or that don't close when tapped against the kitchen counter – these are dead and not edible.

Fold the pieces of foil in half lengthways and divide the butter, vermouth, garlic and mussels between them. Bring the corners of each piece together to close the parcel, leaving a little space in each one so the mussels with have room to open. Pinch the edges of the parcels together to seal.

Put the parcels on a baking sheet and cook in a preheated oven at 200°C (400°F) Gas 6 for 10–12 minutes or until the mussels have opened – check one of the parcels to see.

Put the parcels on warmed plates and serve with crusty bread to mop up the delicious juices. If you like, put coarsely chopped parsley in a bowl and serve separately for people to sprinkle over their mussels when they open the parcels.

seared scallops

with crushed potatoes

12 large scallops, corals removed

1 tablespoon extra virgin olive oil

sea salt and freshly ground black pepper

crushed potatoes

500 g new potatoes, peeled

1 tablespoon extra virgin olive oil

25 g stoned black olives, chopped

1 tablespoon chopped fresh flat leaf parsley

a few drops of truffle oil (optional)

serves 4

With their sweet flesh and subtle hint of the sea, scallops are a real treat. Truffle oil, though expensive, is used sparingly and transforms this dish into something special. If you don't have any truffle oil, use a flavoured oil of your choice.

Cook the potatoes in a saucepan of lightly salted, boiling water until just tender. Drain well and return to the pan. Lightly crush them with a fork, leaving them still a little chunky. Add the olive oil, olives, parsley and a few drops of truffle oil, if using. Season with salt and pepper and stir well.

Put the scallops in a bowl, add the olive oil, salt and pepper. Toss to coat. Sear the scallops on a preheated stove-top grill pan for 1 minute on each side (don't overcook or they will be tough). Remove to a plate and let them rest briefly.

Put a pile of crushed potatoes onto each plate, lay the scallops on top and sprinkle with a few extra drops of truffle oil, if using.

hot wok chilli prawns

Fast stir-frying is great for seafood, which mustn't be overcooked. It's also great for easy entertaining. You can make the salsa and the prawn mixture ahead of time, then all you need are a few minutes to fry the prawns and serve.

1 red chilli

500 g peeled, uncooked tiger prawns, with the tails on

grated zest and juice of 1 unwaxed lime

1 garlic clove, chopped

2 tablespoons sunflower oil

a pinch of sugar

cucumber coriander salsa

½ cucumber, peeled

a bunch of coriander, coarsely chopped

1 tablespoon rice vinegar

1 teaspoon sugar

sea salt and freshly ground black pepper

serves 4

To prepare the chilli, cut it in half lengthways, then scrape out and discard the seeds. Cut each half lengthways into fine strips. Cut the strips crossways into very fine dice. Put the prawns in a bowl and add the chilli, lime zest and juice, garlic, 1 tablespoon of the oil and the sugar and mix.

To make the cucumber coriander salsa, cut the cucumber into slices lengthways, then stack the slices and cut them into strips. Cut the strips crossways into dice. Put the cucumber and coriander in a second bowl, add the rice vinegar and sugar, then mix, adding salt and pepper to taste.

Heat the remaining sunflower oil in a wok over high heat and add half the prawn mixture. Stir-fry for 1–2 minutes until it is pink and cooked. Keep it warm in a very low oven while you stir-fry the remaining prawns.

When cooked, divide the prawns between 4 plates and serve immediately with the cucumber coriander salsa.

salmon tempura

Tempura batter shouldn't be smooth, so mix it very briefly, using chopsticks rather than a fork. Make the batter just before you use it.

2 eggs

150 ml ice-cold sparkling mineral water

115 g plain flour

55 g cornflour

3 tablespoons finely chopped chives

500 g salmon fillet, sliced crossways into 16 finger strips

sunflower oil, for deep-frying

sea salt

chilli sauce

6 tablespoons sesame seeds, toasted in a dry frying pan

3 red chillies, finely diced

2 tablespoons dark soy sauce

1 tablespoon white wine vinegar

1 tablespoon runny honey

a deep-fryer (optional)

serves 4

To make the chilli sauce, put the sesame seeds and chillies in a bowl and add the soy sauce. Add the vinegar and honey. Stir well.

To make the batter, crack the eggs into a bowl. Pour in the sparkling water and mix quickly. Add the flours and stir briefly with chopsticks. Don't overmix – the batter should have lumps. Add the chives and stir briefly.

Pour the oil into a deep-fryer, saucepan or wok and heat. To test the heat of the oil, add a cube of white bread. If it browns in 20 seconds, the oil is ready for cooking. If you have a cooking thermometer, it should read 195°C (385°F).

Dip the salmon pieces into the batter. Add the pieces to the pan, 3 at a time, and fry, in batches, for 2–3 minutes until golden. Remove from the oil, drain on kitchen paper and sprinkle with salt. Serve immediately with the chilli sauce.

roasted salmon
wrapped in prosciutto

4 thin slices Fontina cheese, rind removed

4 salmon fillets, 175 g each, skinned

4 bay leaves

8 thin slices prosciutto

sea salt and freshly ground black pepper

courgette ribbons and pasta

200 g dried pasta

200 g courgettes, very thinly sliced lengthways

finely grated zest and freshly squeezed juice of 1 unwaxed lemon

2 tablespoons extra virgin olive oil

a bunch of chives, finely chopped

a baking sheet, lightly oiled

serves 4

What makes this dish such a joy is that you will have no last-minute dramas with the fish falling to pieces, because the prosciutto not only adds flavour and crispness, it also parcels up the salmon.

Trim the Fontina slices to fit on top of the salmon fillets. Put a bay leaf on top of each fillet, then a slice of the Fontina. Wrap 2 slices of prosciutto around each piece of salmon, so that it is completely covered.

Transfer to the baking sheet and cook in a preheated oven at 200°C (400°F) Gas 6 for 10–15 minutes, depending on the thickness of the salmon fillets.

Meanwhile, cook the pasta in a large saucepan of boiling, salted water until al dente, or according to the directions on the packet. Add the courgette slices to the pasta for the final 3 minutes of cooking.

Put the lemon zest and juice in a bowl, add the oil and mix. Add the chives, salt and pepper. Drain the pasta and courgettes and return them to the pan. Add the lemon juice mixture and toss to coat. Serve with the roasted salmon.

seared swordfish

with avocado and salsa

2 tablespoons olive oil

grated zest and juice of 2 unwaxed limes

4 swordfish steaks

2 large, just-ripe avocados, halved, stoned, peeled and sliced

freshly ground black pepper

salsa

1 small red onion, chopped

1 red chilli, deseeded and very finely chopped

1 large ripe tomato, halved, deseeded and chopped

3 tablespoons extra virgin olive oil

grated zest and juice of 1 unwaxed lime

to serve

1 lime, cut into wedges

a bunch of coriander, chopped

serves 4

Like tuna, swordfish is perfect for grilling – its texture is quite meat-like, so it doesn't flake or fall apart.

Put the oil, lime zest and juice in a small bowl and whisk well. Add plenty of pepper. Put the swordfish steaks in a shallow dish and pour over the oil and lime mixture, making sure the fish is coated on all sides. Cover and refrigerate for up to 1 hour.

Meanwhile, to make the salsa, put the onion, chilli, tomato, oil, lime zest and juice in a bowl. Mix gently, then cover and refrigerate.

Heat a stove-top grill pan to hot and cook the fish for about 2–3 minutes on each side or until just cooked through. Divide the avocado slices and fish between 4 plates, spoon over the salsa, sprinkle with coriander and serve with lime wedges.

peppered tuna steak
with salsa rossa

You can make the salsa rossa in advance – it can be stored in the refrigerator for up to three days – leaving you very little to do when your guests arrive.

6 tablespoons mixed peppercorns, coarsely crushed

6 tuna steaks, 200 g each

1 tablespoon extra virgin olive oil

mixed salad leaves, to serve

salsa rossa

1 large red pepper

1 tablespoon extra virgin olive oil

2 garlic cloves, crushed

2 large ripe tomatoes, peeled and roughly chopped

a small pinch of dried chilli flakes

1 tablespoon dried oregano

1 tablespoon red wine vinegar

sea salt and freshly ground black pepper

serves 6

To make the salsa rossa, grill the pepper until charred all over, then put into a plastic bag and let cool. Remove and discard the skin and seeds, reserving any juices, then chop the flesh.

Put the oil in a frying pan, heat gently, then add the garlic and sauté for 3 minutes. Add the tomatoes, chilli flakes and oregano and simmer gently for 15 minutes. Stir in the pepper and the vinegar and simmer for a further 5 minutes to evaporate any excess liquid.

Transfer to a blender and purée until fairly smooth. Add salt and pepper to taste and let cool. It may be stored in a screw-top jar in the refrigerator for up to 3 days.

Put the crushed peppercorns on a large plate. Brush the tuna steaks with oil, then press the crushed peppercorns into the surface. Preheat a stove-top grill pan or barbecue until hot, add the tuna and cook for 1 minute on each side. Wrap loosely in foil and let rest for 5 minutes before serving with the salsa rossa and a salad of mixed leaves.

saffron fish roast

Roasted vegetables make a delicious base for grilled fish in this recipe. You can roast rather than grill the fish too, but remember that it will take a very short time, so cook it just until the flesh turns opaque.

2 red onions, cut into wedges

2 red peppers, halved, deseeded and each half cut into 3

500 g new potatoes

1 tablespoon olive oil

250 g baby plum tomatoes

500 g thick, skinless cod fillet, cut into 4 chunks

500 g thick, skinless salmon fillet, cut into 4 slices

½ teaspoon rock or sea salt

freshly ground black pepper

1 lemon, cut into wedges, to serve

marinade

a pinch of saffron threads

4 tablespoons finely chopped flat leaf parsley

2 tablespoons extra virgin olive oil

serves 4

Put the saffron in a small bowl, add 3 tablespoons boiling water and set aside to soak.

Put the onions, peppers and potatoes in a large roasting tin. Add the olive oil and salt and pepper to taste and mix well. Roast in a preheated oven at 200°C (400°F) Gas 6 for about 45 minutes until the vegetables are cooked and slightly charred. Add the tomatoes to the tin and roast for a further 5 minutes.

Meanwhile, to make the marinade, put the saffron and its soaking water in a large bowl, add the parsley, oil and pepper and mix. Put the fish in a shallow dish and pour over the marinade. Cover and refrigerate until needed.

Preheat the grill to medium heat. Remove the fish from its marinade and discard the marinade. Put the fish on top of the vegetables in the roasting tin. Sprinkle with the rock or sea salt and cook under the grill for 10–12 minutes, turning the fish once, until the fish is just cooked through.

Divide the fish and vegetables between 4 plates and serve with the lemon wedges.

mediterranean fish stew

Prawn shells are full of flavour and this will seep into the sauce, contributing to its richness. Eat this dish with your fingers and mop up with plenty of crusty fresh bread.

12 mussels

1 large fennel bulb, with leafy tops

2 tablespoons olive oil

2 garlic cloves, crushed

200 ml dry white wine

300 ml fish stock

800 g canned chopped tomatoes

a pinch of sugar

250 g cherry tomatoes, halved

500 g monkfish fillet, cut into 4 cm chunks

12 large, unpeeled, uncooked prawns, heads removed

sea salt and freshly ground black pepper

extra virgin olive oil, to serve

serves 4

Scrub the mussels clean and rinse them in several changes of cold water to remove grit. Pull off the beards or seaweed-like threads and discard any mussels that are cracked or that don't close when tapped against the kitchen counter – these are dead and not edible.

Remove the leafy tops from the fennel bulb, chop them coarsely and set aside. Cut the bulb into quarters, remove and discard the core, then finely chop the bulb.

Heat the oil in a large saucepan or wok. Add the fennel bulb and fry for 5 minutes. Add the garlic and fry for a further 1 minute. Add the wine, stock, canned tomatoes and sugar and stir well. Bring to the boil, then reduce the heat and simmer for 5 minutes. Add the cherry tomatoes and cook for a further 5 minutes. Add plenty of salt and pepper.

Add the monkfish and return to simmering. Stir in the mussels and prawns, cover and cook for about 5 minutes or until the mussels have opened and the fish is cooked.

Ladle the stew into deep plates or bowls. Sprinkle with the fennel tops and olive oil and serve.

traditional fish pie

There may seem to be a lot of mustard in this sauce, but it loses its heat when cooked and you will be left with a delicious flavour which is difficult to place once the poaching liquid has been added.

500 ml milk

750 g smoked or fresh haddock, skinned

275 g unsalted butter

1 tablespoon dry English mustard powder

4 tablespoons plain flour

2 hard-boiled eggs, peeled and quartered

1 kg floury potatoes

sea salt and freshly ground black pepper

a shallow oven dish or casserole

serves 4

Put the milk in a wide saucepan, heat just to boiling point, then add the fish. Turn off the heat and let it poach until opaque. Do not overcook.

Meanwhile, melt 125 g of the butter in another saucepan, then stir in the mustard and flour. Remove from the heat and strain the poaching liquid into the pan.

Arrange the fish and eggs in a shallow oven dish or casserole.

Return the pan to the heat and, whisking vigorously to smooth out any lumps, bring the mixture to the boil. Season with salt and pepper if necessary. (Take care: if you are using smoked fish, it may be salty enough.) Pour the sauce into the casserole and mix carefully with the fish and eggs.

Cook the potatoes in boiling salted water until soft, then drain. Return to the pan. Melt the remaining 150 g butter in a small saucepan. Reserve 4 tablespoons of this butter and stir the remainder into the potatoes. Mash well and season with salt and pepper. Spoon the mixture carefully over the fish, brush generously with the reserved butter and transfer to a preheated oven at 200°C (400°F) Gas 6 for 20 minutes or until nicely browned.

chicken & duck

pan-fried chicken
with creamy beans and leeks

This is a great supper dish for weekday entertaining – simple and quick. The combination of beans and leeks, which is also very good with lamb, makes for a satisfying meal, though if you want something lighter you could serve a simple green salad instead.

4 boneless chicken breasts

25 g butter

1 tablespoon extra virgin olive oil

sea salt and freshly ground black pepper

watercress salad, to serve

mustard and tarragon butter

2 tablespoons chopped fresh tarragon

1 tablespoon wholegrain mustard

125 g softened butter

creamy beans with leeks

50 g butter

2 leeks, finely chopped

1 garlic clove, crushed

2 teaspoons chopped fresh rosemary

800 g canned flageolet beans, drained, rinsed and drained again

300 ml vegetable stock

4 tablespoons double cream

serves 4

To make the mustard and tarragon butter, beat the tarragon leaves into the butter with the mustard. Roll, wrap and freeze.

To cook the beans and leeks, melt the butter in a saucepan, add the leeks, garlic and rosemary and fry gently for 5 minutes until softened but not golden.

Add the beans, stir once, then pour in the stock. Bring to the boil, cover and simmer for 15 minutes. Remove the lid, stir in the cream, add salt and pepper to taste, then simmer, uncovered, for a further 5 minutes until the sauce has thickened. Set aside while you prepare the chicken.

Season the chicken with salt and pepper. Heat the butter and oil in a frying pan and, as soon as the butter stops foaming, cook the chicken, skin side down, for 4 minutes. Turn it over and cook for a further 4 minutes.

Top each breast with 1–2 slices of the mustard and tarragon butter and let rest for 2–3 minutes in a low oven. Serve with the beans and leeks and a simple watercress salad.

These mini chickens can be roasted in about 40 minutes. To make sure they are cooked through, push a skewer into the leg meat right down to the bone. If the juices run clear, the birds are cooked. If not, return them to the oven for a little longer.

garlic-roasted poussins

2 whole heads of garlic, separated

2 large poussins

½ lemon

4 sprigs of thyme

50 g butter, softened

100 ml white wine

300 ml chicken stock

1 tablespoon plain flour

sea salt and freshly ground black pepper

serves 4

Boil the garlic cloves in a saucepan of lightly salted water for 15 minutes, drain and pat dry (this can be done ahead of time).

Meanwhile, wash the poussins, pat them dry and rub all over with the cut lemon. Chop the lemon into small chunks and put them and the thyme into the body cavities. Season generously with salt and pepper and rub the birds all over with 40 g of the butter.

Put 1 garlic clove into each bird, then put the rest in a large roasting tin. Sit the poussins on top and roast in a preheated oven at 200°C (400°F) Gas 6 for 40 minutes. Transfer the poussins and garlic cloves to a large plate, wrap loosely in foil and let rest for 10 minutes.

Meanwhile, to make a gravy, spoon off any excess fat from the roasting tin. Add the wine, bring to the boil and scrape any sediments into the wine. Boil until reduced by two-thirds. Add the stock and boil for 5 minutes or until reduced by half. Put the remaining butter and the flour into a bowl and beat until smooth. Gradually whisk into the gravy, stirring over gentle heat until thickened.

Serve the poussins with the garlic and gravy.

coq au vin

This is France's most famous stew. To be authentic, it should contain mushrooms, bacon lardons and caramelized baby onions.

1 large chicken, preferably free range or
corn-fed, cut into serving pieces

leaves from 1 sprig of thyme,
finely chopped

50 g butter

60 ml brandy

1 bottle rich red wine, 750 ml

750 ml chicken stock

4 tomatoes, skinned and deseeded,
or 2 teaspoons tomato purée

2 garlic cloves, crushed

1 bay leaf

125 g smoked bacon, in the piece,
cut into lardons

125 g butter

125 g button mushrooms, sliced

12 baby onions

sea salt and freshly ground
black pepper

roux

50 g butter

2 tablespoons plain flour

a large flameproof casserole

serves 4

Season the chicken pieces with salt and pepper and sprinkle with the thyme leaves. Put the butter in a large, flameproof casserole and heat until it begins to brown. Add the chicken pieces to the casserole and sauté, skin side down, until golden brown.

Remove the casserole from the heat, pour over the brandy and set it alight if you wish; otherwise let it boil away so the alcohol evaporates. Using tongs or a slotted spoon, remove the chicken pieces to a plate and keep them warm. Pour the wine into the casserole, bring to the boil and reduce to 3 tablespoons. Add the tomatoes or purée, garlic and bay leaf and mix well.

To make the roux, heat the butter in a small frying pan, add the flour and cook, stirring, until the mixture is a pale brown. Stir it into the wine mixture.

Reserve 250 ml of the stock, then stir the remainder into the casserole and bring to the boil. Add the chicken pieces and any juices that have run onto the plate. Season to taste with salt and pepper, cover with a lid and cook in a preheated oven at 180°C (350°F) Gas 4 for 40 minutes or until the chicken juices run clear when pricked with a fork.

Meanwhile, bring a saucepan of water to the boil, add the bacon, boil for 1 minute, then drain. Add the bacon into the casserole halfway through the cooking time. Put 75 g of the serving butter in a small frying pan, add the mushrooms and sauté for 5 minutes. Transfer to the casserole for the last 5 minutes of cooking time.

Put the remaining butter in the frying pan, add the onions and sauté until browned, about 5 minutes. Add the reserved 250 ml chicken stock, bring to the boil and simmer until tender and the stock has been absorbed, about 10 minutes. Serve on warmed plates, topping each chicken piece with a share of the mushrooms, bacon and golden onions.

stir-fried chicken with greens

There won't be many people who don't appreciate this dish. Stir-fried also effectively means 'steam-stirred', because the vegetables are mostly cooked in the aromatic steam. Use a sweet chilli sauce, not a fiery Southeast Asian version.

175 g green beans, halved

2 tablespoons peanut oil

500 g chicken breasts, cubed, or 3 large skinless, boneless breasts cut into 5 cm strips or cubes

5 cm fresh ginger, shredded

2 garlic cloves, sliced

250 g broccoli, broken into tiny florets

8 spring onions, halved crossways

1 red or yellow pepper, deseeded and cut into strips

6 tablespoons chicken stock or water

2 tablespoons sweet chilli sauce

1 tablespoon light soy sauce

50 g mangetout (snowpeas), trimmed and washed

50 g sugar snap peas, trimmed and washed

100 g baby bok choy leaves, trimmed and washed

noodles or rice, to serve

serves 4

To blanch the beans, bring a saucepan of water to the boil, add the beans and boil for 2–3 minutes until they turn bright green. Drain, run under cold water and drain again.

Put the oil in a wok and heat until very hot but not smoking. Alternatively, use a large, preferably non-stick, frying pan. Add the chicken and stir-fry over a high heat for 2 minutes, then add the ginger and garlic and stir-fry for a further 2 minutes.

Add the broccoli, spring onions, green beans, sliced pepper and chicken stock or water. Cover and cook for a further 2–3 minutes. Stir in the chilli sauce and soy sauce. Toss the still-wet mangetout, sugar snap peas and bok choy leaves on top. Cover and cook for 1–2 minutes.

Toss well and serve while the tastes and colours are still vivid and the textures crisp. Accompany with noodles or rice.

2 kg chicken pieces, trimmed

4 tablespoons sesame oil

100 ml light soy sauce

4 garlic cloves, crushed and very finely chopped

1 teaspoon chilli powder

5 spring onions, very finely chopped

freshly ground black pepper

to serve

500 g dried egg noodles

1 teaspoon black sesame seeds (optional)

an ovenproof dish

serves **8**

korean chicken

This traditional Korean dish which looks and tastes great is so simple to make. You will need to marinate the chicken the night before, but then you just transfer it from the fridge to the oven when you are ready to cook.

Put the chicken into an ovenproof dish, add the sesame oil, soy sauce, garlic, chilli powder, spring onions and black pepper to taste. Mix well, cover and chill overnight in the refrigerator.

Uncover the chicken and cook in a preheated oven at 180°C (350°F) Gas 4 for 30 minutes. Reduce to 140°C (275°F) Gas 1 and cook for a further 40 minutes.

Meanwhile, cook the noodles according to the directions on the packet. Drain, then serve the chicken and noodles, sprinkled with the black sesame seeds, if using.

hot chicken tikka platter
with yoghurt

Your friends will be most impressed when you serve up your own version of this popular Indian dish.

3 boneless, skinless chicken breasts, cut into strips

freshly squeezed juice of 1 lemon

4 tablespoons tikka or mild curry paste

2 garlic cloves, crushed

250 g French beans

1 tablespoon oil

125 g baby spinach leaves

freshly ground black pepper

to serve

a bunch of coriander, coarsely chopped (optional)

150 g Greek yoghurt

serves 4

Put the chicken strips in a large bowl and sprinkle with the lemon juice. Add the tikka or curry paste and garlic. Mix well. (If time allows, marinate in the refrigerator for 30 minutes.)

Heat a large wok or frying pan. Add the chicken with its marinade and cook for 5–7 minutes until the chicken is opaque and cooked all the way through. Add pepper to taste.

Meanwhile, to blanch the beans, bring a saucepan of water to the boil, add the beans and boil for 2–3 minutes until they turn bright green. Drain, run under cold water and drain again. Heat a second wok or large frying pan. Add the oil and, when hot, add the drained beans. Remove from the heat and add the spinach leaves. Toss to mix.

To serve, pile the spinach and beans in the centre of a large serving dish. Top with the hot chicken, sprinkle with coriander, if using, and serve with Greek yoghurt.

chicken 'panini'
with mozzarella

Panini is the Italian word for little sandwiches, usually toasted. Here, instead of bread, try toasting (or grilling) chicken breast fillets stuffed with basil and mozzarella – melted, gooey and delicious!

250 g mozzarella cheese
4 large, skinless, boneless chicken breasts
8 large basil leaves
2 garlic cloves, thinly sliced
1 tablespoon olive oil
sea salt and freshly ground black pepper

to serve

salsa rossa (page 125)
basil leaves

serves 4

Cut the mozzarella into 8 thick slices and set aside.

Put the chicken breasts onto a board and, using a sharp knife, cut horizontally into the thickness without cutting all the way through. Open out flat and season the insides with a little salt and pepper.

Put 2 basil leaves, a few garlic slices and 2 slices of cheese into each breast, then fold back over, pressing firmly together. Secure with cocktail sticks.

Brush the parcels with a little oil and cook on a preheated barbecue or stove-top grill pan for about 8 minutes on each side until the cheese is beginning to ooze at the sides and the chicken is cooked.

Serve hot with the salsa rossa and sprinkled with a few basil leaves.

honeyed duck
with mango salsa

4 small to medium duck breasts,
with skin on

1 tablespoon soy sauce

1 tablespoon honey

sea salt

mango salsa

1 large ripe mango

1 orange pepper, halved, deseeded
and diced

6 spring onions, finely sliced

2 tablespoons olive oil

grated zest and juice of
1 unwaxed orange

freshly squeezed juice of 1 lime

4 sprigs of coriander

serves 4

Duck always works well with fruit and this recipe is also good with nectarines. Pricking the duck skin stops it shrinking as it cooks, while the honey-soy mixture produces a delicious, crackly skin.

Cut the sides off the mango in 4 slabs, from top to bottom, and discard the stone and surrounding flesh. With a small, sharp knife, cut a criss-cross pattern into the flesh of each piece, down to the skin. Push the skin with your thumbs to invert and scrape off the cubes of flesh with a knife.

Put the mango in a bowl with the remaining salsa ingredients and set aside to develop the flavours. Meanwhile, preheat the oven to 230°C (450°F) Gas 8.

Prick the duck skin all over with a fork and rub with a little salt. Transfer the duck breasts to a wire rack set over a roasting tin (this will allow the excess fat to drip away).

Put the soy sauce and honey in a small bowl and mix well. Spread the mixture over the duck skin. Transfer to the oven and roast for 15–20 minutes until the duck is just cooked but still pink in the middle and the skin is well browned and crisp. Remove from the oven and let the duck rest for 5 minutes before carving.

Carve the duck breasts crossways into slices and serve with the mango salsa.

meat & game

gremolata pork
with lemon spinach

4 boneless pork chops, 75 g each

1 tablespoon basil oil

50 g ciabatta bread, torn into pieces

4 tablespoons coarsely chopped flat leaf parsley

grated zest of 1 unwaxed lemon

2 tablespoons olive oil

freshly ground black pepper

lemon spinach

250 g young spinach leaves, washed, dried and thinly sliced

1 tablespoon extra virgin olive oil, plus extra for serving

freshly squeezed juice of ½ lemon

serves 4

In this recipe, which demonstrates one of the great advantages of shallow-frying, pork chops are coated in breadcrumbs and then fried gently to give a crisp outside while the meat remains tender inside.

Trim any excess fat from the pork chops, leaving a thin layer around the meat. Put each chop between 2 pieces of clingfilm and, using a rolling pin, beat to ½ cm thickness. Remove and discard the clingfilm and put the pork in a shallow dish. Add the basil oil and sprinkle with pepper. Turn to coat, cover and refrigerate for 2 hours.

To make the breadcrumbs, put the ciabatta pieces in a food processor and pulse to coarse crumbs. Put the breadcrumbs, parsley and lemon zest in a bowl and mix. Add black pepper to taste. Transfer to a plate and coat the pork with the crumb mixture, pressing gently until covered on both sides.

Heat the oil in a large frying pan, add the pork and cook for about 2 minutes on each side or until the breadcrumbs are golden and the pork is cooked through.

Put the spinach in a large bowl, add the olive oil and lemon juice and toss to coat. Put a mound of spinach on each plate and top with the pork. Drizzle with the olive oil, season with pepper and serve.

italian pork tenderloin
with fennel and garlic

There are two ways to cook the pork. If you're in a rush, use the fast-roast method, a favourite with many modern cooks. Alternatively, use the slow-cooking method, which keeps the pork moister and more tender. Directions for both are given below.

2 pork tenderloins, about 400–500 g each, trimmed

seasoning

2 teaspoons fennel seeds

½ teaspoon coarse salt

5 black peppercorns

2 garlic cloves, crushed

6 tablespoons extra virgin olive oil

serves 4

To make the seasoning, grind the fennel seeds, salt and peppercorns in a mortar. Mash in the garlic and olive oil to form a paste. Make a few light slashes in each tenderloin and put onto a roasting tray. Rub the seasoning oil all over the pork and pour any that remains on top.

To fast-roast, cook on the middle shelf of a preheated oven at 220°C (425°F) Gas 7 for 20 minutes or until the internal temperature registers 65°C (150°F) on an instant-read thermometer, or until there are no pink juices when you pierce the meat with a skewer. Baste the pork several times while roasting.

If following the slower method, cook in a preheated oven at 160°C (325°F) Gas 3 for about 45 minutes or until done, as above. Baste several times.

For both methods, let the pork rest for 10 minutes before slicing and serving.

burmese pork hinleh

3 tablespoons peanut or vegetable oil

750 g well-trimmed boneless pork sparerib, sliced into chunks

500 ml beef stock

hinleh (curry) paste

4–6 red bird's-eye chillies, deseeded and chopped

5 garlic cloves, quartered

½ onion, coarsely chopped

5 cm fresh ginger, peeled and grated

¼ teaspoon ground turmeric

2 cm fresh galangal, peeled and grated (see recipe introduction)*

1 stalk of lemongrass, outer leaves discarded, the remainder very finely chopped

3 anchovies in oil, drained and finely chopped, plus a dash of fish sauce

to serve

a handful of Thai basil or coriander

2 red bird's-eye chillies, thinly sliced lengthways

375 g rice

serves 4

*Fresh galangal is available from Asian shops and markets.

This curry is a Burmese speciality and doesn't include the coconut milk so typical of Southeast Asian cooking. It does use three root spices from the same family: turmeric, ginger and galangal. In Burma and throughout Asia all three are used fresh, but in the West turmeric root is rarely available, so the ground form must be used. If you can't get fresh galangal, use more fresh ginger.

To make the hinleh paste, put all the ingredients in a blender and grind to a paste, adding a dash of water to let the blades run. Alternatively, use a mortar and pestle.

Heat the oil in a large saucepan and add the paste. Stir-fry for several minutes. Add the pork and stir-fry to seal. Add the stock, bring to the boil, reduce the heat and simmer gently, stirring occasionally, for 40–45 minutes until cooked through but very tender.

Meanwhile, boil the rice according to the instructions on the packet.

Sprinkle the curry with the herbs and chilli and serve with the boiled rice.

braised lamb shanks

with orange and marmalade

Meat cooked on the bone has a very different texture from the boned type, where the meat can shrink back unimpeded into a tight ball. Here the lamb remains stretched as it cooks and has a tender, more open texture.

4 lamb shanks

4 tablespoons olive oil

3 garlic cloves, sliced

freshly squeezed juice of 2 oranges, about 250 ml

125 ml dry white wine

zest of 1 unwaxed lemon

3 tablespoons bitter orange marmalade

125 ml hot chicken stock or hot water

sea salt and freshly ground black pepper

a flameproof casserole

serves 4

Preheat a grill until very hot. Brush the shanks with 3 tablespoons of the oil and season well, then grill, turning them as necessary until well browned all over.

Heat the remaining oil in a flameproof casserole, add the garlic and brown gently without burning. Add the shanks, orange juice, wine and lemon zest. Bring to the boil on top of the stove, cover with a lid, then transfer to a preheated oven and cook at 180°C (350°F) Gas 4 for 1 hour or until the meat pulls away from the bone.

Using a slotted spoon, transfer the shanks to a plate or bowl and keep them warm in a low oven. Transfer the casserole to the top of the stove over a medium heat.

Add the marmalade to the casserole, stir until well blended, bring to the boil and simmer until the liquid has been reduced to a coating glaze.

Return the shanks to the casserole and turn in the glaze until well coated. Serve on warmed plates. Add the stock to the casserole, stir to scrape up the flavoured bits left in the bottom, then spoon over the shanks. Serve with your choice of steamed vegetables and mashed sweet potatoes.

roasted pheasant breasts
with bacon, shallots and mushrooms

Depending on size, you may need two breasts per person –
this is something you can decide when shopping. Cooking a
whole pheasant is more economical and will serve between
two and three people, but involves all that last-minute carving
and it never looks as good.

6 plump pheasant breasts

12 slices smoked, rindless bacon

6 sprigs of thyme

3 fresh bay leaves, halved

25 g butter

1 tablespoon olive oil

12 shallots

100 ml dry sherry

6 portobello mushrooms, quartered

6 thick slices French bread

200 g watercress

sea salt and freshly cracked black pepper

serves 6

Remove the skin from the pheasant breasts and discard
it. Wrap 2 slices of bacon around each breast, inserting a
sprig of thyme and half a bay leaf between the pheasant
and the bacon.

Put the butter and oil in a large roasting tin and set on
top of the stove over high heat. Add the pheasant breasts,
shallots, sherry, mushrooms, salt and pepper. Turn the
pheasant breasts until they are well coated. Cook at the
top of a preheated oven at 190°C (375°F) Gas 5 for
25 minutes.

Remove from the oven and let rest for 5 minutes.

Put the bread onto 6 plates, then add the watercress,
mushrooms, shallots and pheasant. Spoon over any
cooking juices and serve.

venison sausages
with port and cranberry ragout

You can make this with any good-quality sausages, but the gamy venison goes particularly well with the rich, red sauce.

2 large leeks, cut into 5 mm slices

25 g butter

1 tablespoon plain flour

1 tablespoon sugar

300 ml red wine

3 tablespoons port

150 ml chicken or vegetable stock

a large sprig of rosemary

8 good-quality sausages, preferably venison

250 g fresh or frozen cranberries

sea salt and freshly ground black pepper

Classic Creamy Mashed Potatoes (page 109), to serve

serves 4

Rinse the leeks well in a bowl of cold water to remove any grit or dirt, then drain in a sieve. Melt the butter in a large saucepan. Add the leeks and gently fry over medium heat, stirring frequently, for 8–10 minutes until softened and slightly golden.

Preheat the grill to a medium setting.

Add the flour to the pan of fried leeks and cook, stirring, for 1 minute. Add the sugar, wine, port, stock, rosemary and plenty of salt and pepper. Bring to the boil, reduce the heat and simmer for 15–20 minutes.

Meanwhile, cook the sausages under a preheated hot grill, turning frequently, for 15–20 minutes until browned all over and cooked all the way through.

Add the cranberries to the leek mixture and simmer for a further 5–6 minutes until they begin to soften and pop. Add salt, pepper and sugar to taste.

Serve the sausages with the port and cranberry ragout and the mashed potatoes.

This combination of Vietnamese marinated beef, crème fraîche, steamed sweet potatoes and spicy chilli tomato relish is a terrific party piece.

pan-grilled vietnamese beef
with crème fraîche and chilli tomato relish

4 slices fillet steak, each about 3 cm thick

4 small orange sweet potatoes, peeled and cut crossways into 2 cm thick slices

marinade

2 tablespoons fish sauce

2 tablespoons mirin (Japanese rice wine)

1 tablespoon toasted sesame oil

grated zest and juice of 1 unwaxed lime

chilli tomato relish

250 g ripe tomatoes, skinned and chopped

250 g red peppers, peeled and chopped

6 red chillies, deseeded and chopped

7.5 cm piece fresh ginger, peeled and grated

2 tablespoons salt

200 g sugar

6 tablespoons sherry vinegar

to serve

salad leaves

4 heaped tablespoons crème fraîche

serves 4

To make the chilli tomato relish, put all the ingredients in a food processor and pulse until coarsely chopped. Transfer to a saucepan, bring to the boil, skim off the foam, then reduce the heat and simmer for 30 minutes. Pour into hot sterilized jars (page 4), seal and let cool. Use immediately or store in the refrigerator: it will keep for 2 weeks.

Mix the marinade ingredients in a shallow dish. Add the beef, cover and set aside for at least 15 minutes. Turn over and marinate for at least another 15 minutes. Alternatively, marinate in the refrigerator overnight.

Heat a stove-top grill pan to medium-hot. Add the beef and cook for about 2 minutes on each side. The meat should be brown outside and rare in the middle. If you want it medium, cook for another 2 minutes.

Meanwhile, steam the sweet potatoes until tender. Alternatively, boil in salted water, then drain.

To serve, put a handful of leaves on each plate, add a steak and a tumble of sweet potatoes, then 1 tablespoon crème fraîche and 1–2 tablespoons chilli tomato relish.

Steak always turns dinner into a special treat. Make the blue cheese butter ahead of time, then you can prepare the rest of the dish in a matter of minutes.

steak with blue cheese butter

4 fillet steaks, 200 g each

sea salt and freshly ground black pepper

oil, for pan-frying (optional)

baby spinach salad, to serve

blue cheese butter

50 g unsalted butter, softened

50 g soft blue cheese, such as Gorgonzola

25 g walnuts, finely ground in a blender

2 tablespoons chopped fresh parsley

serves 4

To make the blue cheese butter, put the butter, cheese, walnuts and parsley in a bowl and beat well. Season to taste. Form into a log, wrap in foil and chill for about 30 minutes.

Lightly season the steaks and cook on a preheated barbecue or pan-fry in a little oil for 3 minutes on each side for rare or 4–5 minutes for medium to well done.

Cut the butter into 8 slices. Put 2 slices of butter onto each cooked steak, wrap loosely with foil and let rest for 5 minutes.

Serve the steaks with a salad of baby spinach.

steak and mushroom pie

Nothing beats a good home-made pie with tender pieces of meat in a delicious gravy. This one is topped with simple-to-make crisp suet pastry and is a sure winner.

filling

3 tablespoons olive oil

2 onions, chopped

750 g braising steak, cubed

200 g button mushrooms

1 tablespoon flour

½ teaspoon dried mixed herbs

1 teaspoon Worcestershire sauce

1 teaspoon English mustard, or Dijon

400 ml beef stock

sea salt and freshly ground black pepper

suet pastry

250 g self-raising flour

125 g shredded suet or shortening

a 1.2 litre pie dish

serves 4

To make the filling, heat the olive oil in a large frying pan, add the onions and fry until softened and translucent. Transfer to a plate. Add a little more oil to the pan if needed, then add the meat and sauté until browned and sealed. Add the mushrooms and fry for about 5 minutes, then sprinkle in the flour and mix well to absorb all the oil.

Return the onions to the pan and add the mixed herbs, Worcestershire sauce, mustard, salt and pepper. Slowly pour in the stock, blending well. Bring to the boil, then lower the heat and simmer for 1½ hours.

When the meat is almost cooked, make the pastry. Sift the flour into a bowl, add the suet or shortening, salt and pepper and mix well. Add about 5 tablespoons water and mix with a round-bladed knife until the mixture forms a dough. A little more water may be needed, but take care not to add too much because it will make the pastry difficult to handle.

Transfer the cooked meat to the pie dish and set aside to cool.

Roll out the pastry to a disc larger than the pie dish. Wet the lip of the dish, then cut thin strips of pastry from the trimmings and press onto the lip. Dampen this pastry lip, then lay the rolled pastry over the pie and flute the edge with your fingers to seal. Trim and make a small hole in the centre.

Bake in a preheated oven at 220°C (425°F) Gas 7 for 35 minutes until golden brown.

Stews aren't difficult: just put them on to cook and they look after themselves. This one actually makes a useful two-course meal if you serve some of the juices poured over pasta as a starter, then have the meat proper as your main course. The stew improves if it is made the day before and reheated.

boeuf en daube

1 kg beef, such as shoulder or topside, cut into 1 cm slices

4 tablespoons extra virgin olive oil

4 garlic cloves, sliced

125 g thick-cut unsmoked bacon, diced, or bacon lardons, cubed

3 carrots, halved lengthways

12–16 baby onions, peeled

6 plum tomatoes, skinned and thickly sliced

zest of 1 unwaxed orange

a bunch of fresh herbs, such as parsley, thyme, bay leaf and rosemary, tied together with kitchen string

60 g walnut halves

250 ml robust red wine

2 tablespoons Cognac or brandy

150 ml beef stock or water

15 cm square of pork or bacon rind (optional)

chopped fresh parsley, to serve (optional)

a large flameproof casserole

serves 4–6

Cut the beef into pieces about the size of 'half a postcard', as Elizabeth David advised – in other words, 6 cm squares. Heat the oil in a large, flameproof casserole, add the garlic, bacon, carrots and onions and sauté for 4–5 minutes or until aromatic. Remove from the casserole. Put a layer of meat into the casserole, then add half the sautéed vegetable mixture and a second layer of meat. Add the remaining vegetable mixture, the tomatoes, orange zest, herbs and walnuts.

Put the wine in a small saucepan and bring to the boil. Add the Cognac or brandy and warm for a few seconds, shaking the pan a little to let the alcohol cook off. Pour the hot liquids over the meat with just enough stock or water so that it's barely covered. Put the pork rind, if using, on top.

Heat the casserole until simmering, then cover with foil and a lid and simmer gently for 2 hours or until the meat is fork tender and the juices rich and sticky.

The dish can also be cooked in the oven. Just bring to the boil over a high heat, reduce to a simmer, cover with foil, replace the lid and cook in the oven at 150°C (300°F) Gas 2 for 2½ hours or until very tender.

Remove and discard the pork rind, which will have given a velvety quality to the sauce. Sprinkle with chopped parsley, if using. Serve hot on its own or with accompaniments such as pasta, Classic Creamy Mashed Potatoes (page 109) or boiled rice.

moroccan lamb tagine

1 kg boneless shoulder of lamb, trimmed of about half its fat and cut into 5 cm chunks

600 ml chicken stock

2 tablespoons olive oil

1 large onion, coarsely chopped

4 garlic cloves, chopped

1 tablespoon ground cumin

1 tablespoon ground coriander

1 tablespoon hot paprika

400 g canned chopped tomatoes

1 cinnamon stick, broken in half

175 g dried apricots

½ teaspoon freshly ground black pepper

3 large pieces of unwaxed orange zest

orange relish

2 oranges, separated into segments

1 red onion, chopped

1 red chilli, finely chopped

leaves from a bunch of coriander

1 tablespoon mint leaves, thinly sliced

to serve

50 g pine nuts, lightly toasted in a dry frying pan

couscous

serves 4

A tagine is a North African stew cooked in a tall, conical pot of the same name. It is traditionally made over an open fire, but it also works well in the oven or in a wok or sauté pan on top of the stove.

Heat a large, non-stick sauté pan or wok until hot. Add half the lamb chunks and sear on all sides until brown. Using a slotted spoon, remove the from the pan, put on a plate and set aside. Add about 100 ml of the chicken stock to the pan. Stir with a wooden spoon to remove all the flavourful sediment from the bottom, then pour out into a jug and reserve. Add the remaining lamb to the pan and sear until brown, repeating the chicken stock process.

Return the pan to the heat and add the oil. When hot, add the onion and fry gently for about 10 minutes until golden. Add the garlic and fry for a further 2 minutes. Add the cumin, ground coriander and paprika to the pan and fry for a further 1 minute. Add the reserved browned lamb and the tomatoes, cinnamon, apricots, pepper, orange zest and remaining stock. Bring to the boil and cover with a lid. Reduce the heat and simmer very gently for about 2 hours until the meat is meltingly tender. Alternatively, cover with a lid and transfer to a preheated oven and cook at 150°C (300°F) Gas 2 for about 2 hours or until the meat is very tender.

To make the orange relish, put the orange segments, onion, chilli, coriander and mint in a bowl and mix. Serve the tagine sprinkled with pine nuts, accompanied by the orange relish and couscous.

pasta, rice & noodles

sicilian spaghetti

Good olive oil and Mediterranean vegetables produce an easy, substantial pasta dish. No long simmering here: the tiny tomato halves are oven-roasted and the cubes of aubergine salted, then sautéed, to intensify the flavour. Handfuls of basil add the final flourish.

1 aubergine, about 350 g, cut into 1 cm cubes

500 g mini plum tomatoes, halved and deseeded

125 ml extra virgin olive oil

125 ml tomato juice or crushed tomatoes

2 garlic cloves, chopped

a large handful of basil leaves

400 g dried pasta, such as spaghettini or penne

sea salt and freshly ground black pepper

a baking sheet

serves 4

Put the aubergine in a non-metal bowl, then add 1 teaspoon salt and set aside while you cook the tomatoes.

Pack the tomatoes, cut side up, on a baking sheet, then sprinkle with salt and 2 tablespoons of the oil. Roast in a preheated oven at 230°C (450°F) Gas 8 for 10 minutes or until wilted and aromatic.

Drain the aubergine and pat dry with kitchen paper. Put 4 tablespoons of the olive oil in a non-stick frying pan and heat gently. Add the aubergine and cook, stirring, over high heat until frizzled and soft, about 8 minutes. Add the roasted tomato halves, tomato juice or crushed tomatoes, garlic and black pepper. Cook, stirring, for 2–3 minutes, then tear up most of the basil leaves, add to the pan and stir.

Meanwhile, bring a large saucepan of water to the boil. Add a pinch of salt, then add the pasta when the fried and roasted vegetables are half cooked. Cook the pasta according to the instructions on the packet.

Drain the cooked pasta, return it to the saucepan and toss in the remaining olive oil. Divide between 4 warmed bowls, spoon over the sauce, sprinkle with a few basil leaves and serve.

pasta with melted ricotta and herby parmesan sauce

Pasta is the archetypal easy food. This one is fast and fresh, with the ricotta melting into the hot pasta and coating it like a creamy sauce. The pine nuts give it crunch, while the herbs lend it authentic flavour.

350 g dried penne or other pasta
6 tablespoons extra virgin olive oil
100 g pine nuts
125 g rocket leaves, chopped
2 tablespoons chopped fresh parsley
2 tablespoons chopped fresh basil
250 g fresh ricotta cheese, mashed
50 g freshly grated Parmesan cheese
sea salt and freshly ground black pepper

serves 4

Bring a large saucepan of water to the boil. Add a pinch of salt, then the pasta, and cook until al dente, or according to the timings on the packet.

Meanwhile, heat the olive oil in a frying pan, add the pine nuts and fry gently until golden. Set aside.

Drain the cooked pasta, reserving 4 tablespoons of the cooking liquid, and return both to the pan. Add the pine nuts and their olive oil, the rocket, the herbs, the ricotta, half the Parmesan and plenty of black pepper. Stir until evenly coated.

Serve in warmed bowls, with the remaining cheese sprinkled on top.

herbed tagliatelle
with prawn skewers

A lovely summery dish which makes the most of garden herbs. Serve the prawns on skewers for a sense of occasion (this also makes them easier to turn while cooking), though they can be cooked separately and added just before serving.

350 g dried pasta, such as tagliatelle, linguine or fettuccine

20 uncooked tiger prawns, peeled with tails on

2 garlic cloves, crushed

½ teaspoon crushed dried chillies

4 tablespoons olive oil

1 lemon, cut into 4 wedges

1 teaspoon chopped fresh rosemary

2 tablespoons chopped fresh flat leaf parsley

1 tablespoon snipped fresh chives

a handful of rocket

sea salt and freshly ground black pepper

4 wooden skewers, soaked in water for 30 minutes

serves 4

Bring a large saucepan of water to the boil. Add a pinch of salt, then the pasta, and cook until al dente or according to the timings on the packet.

Meanwhile, put the prawns in a bowl and add the garlic, dried chillies, 1 tablespoon of the oil and salt and pepper to taste. Mix well, then thread 5 prawns onto each skewer.

Preheat a stove-top grill pan until hot. Add the prawn skewers and cook for 3 minutes on each side until pink and cooked through. Remove and keep them warm in a low oven. Add the lemon wedges to the pan and cook quickly for 30 seconds on each side.

Drain the pasta and return it to the warm pan. Add the remaining oil, rosemary, parsley, chives and rocket, then season with salt and pepper to taste. Toss gently, then divide between 4 warmed bowls. Top each with a prawn skewer and a lemon wedge for squeezing, then serve.

chicken and asparagus spaghetti

This is a one-pot-wonder, with a great combination of clean and fresh flavours. The spaghetti absorbs the rich stock, which means it tastes good as well as looking fantastic. Try this method using other boneless cuts of meat.

2 large tomatoes

300 g dried spaghetti

4 chicken breasts, 100 g each

300 g asparagus, trimmed

200 g fine green beans

4 tablespoons olive oil, plus extra to serve

75 g black olives, stoned and chopped

sea salt and freshly ground black pepper

fresh shavings of Parmesan cheese, to serve

serves 4

Cut a cross in the top of each tomato, put in a bowl and cover with boiling water. Drain after 30 seconds, then skin and chop.

Bring a large saucepan of water to the boil, add a pinch of salt then the spaghetti. Stir, then put the chicken breasts on top of the spaghetti. Cover with a lid and simmer for 8 minutes, then add the asparagus and beans. Replace the lid and cook for a further 3 minutes, until the spaghetti and chicken are cooked. Drain, reserving the cooking liquid for a soup or sauce.

Transfer the chicken to a carving board and cover loosely with foil. Return the spaghetti, asparagus and beans to the saucepan over medium heat and add the oil, olives, tomatoes, salt and pepper. Cook, stirring constantly, for 2 minutes, then transfer to warmed serving plates. Slice the chicken and arrange on top of the spaghetti. Top with Parmesan shavings, drizzle with olive oil, sprinkle with salt and pepper, then serve.

classic lasagne

500 g dried lasagne

300 g mozzarella cheese, drained and diced

4 tablespoons freshly grated Parmesan cheese

sea salt and freshly ground black pepper

bolognese sauce

10 g dried porcini mushrooms, rinsed

1 tablespoon olive oil

1 onion, finely chopped

500 g beef mince

50 g Parma ham, coarsely chopped

100 ml Marsala or sherry

700 ml tomato passata

white sauce

1 litre milk

1 small garlic clove

50 g butter

50 g plain flour

a baking dish, about 30 x 20 x 7 cm

serves 8

Lasagne does take a while to prepare, but you can do everything ahead of time and then put it in the oven when you are ready. Your grateful guests will tell you it's well worth the effort!

To make the bolognese sauce, put the porcini in a bowl, cover with boiling water and set aside for 20 minutes until softened. Heat the oil in a large saucepan, add the onion and cook for 2 minutes. Add the beef mince and Parma ham and cook for 3–4 minutes, stirring until evenly browned. Drain the porcini, chop them, then add to the pan with the Marsala or sherry and passata. Cover and simmer for 1 hour, stirring occasionally, until rich and dark. Add salt and pepper to taste.

To make the white sauce, put the milk and garlic into a small saucepan and heat gently until warm. Melt the butter in a separate saucepan, then stir in the flour and cook for 1 minute. Gradually add the warm milk, stirring constantly to make a smooth sauce. Bring to the boil, then simmer for 2–3 minutes. Discard the garlic clove, then add salt and pepper to taste.

Put 3–4 tablespoons of the bolognese sauce in the baking dish, spread evenly across the base of the dish and cover with a layer of lasagne. Spoon over some white sauce and a few pieces of mozzarella and continue adding layers, starting with another layer of bolognese sauce and finishing with the white sauce and mozzarella, until all the ingredients have been used. Sprinkle with freshly ground black pepper and Parmesan, then bake in a preheated oven at 190°C (375°F) Gas 5 for 30 minutes until the top is crusty and golden.

couscous
with roasted chicken and vegetables

8 small chicken pieces

2 onions, cut into wedges

4 garlic cloves

1 aubergine, cut into chunks

2 courgettes, sliced

100 g frozen peas

leaves from a bunch of flat leaf parsley, chopped

125 g couscous

a pinch of saffron threads

olive oil, for roasting

sea salt and freshly ground black pepper

serves 4

Couscous is extremely easy to cook. In this recipe saffron is added to the boiling water which not only adds a touch of luxury, but also gives the dish an attractive colour.

Trim the chicken of any excess fat and arrange on a heavy-based, lightly oiled roasting tin. Cook in a preheated oven at 190°C (375°F) Gas 5 for 10 minutes.

Remove the chicken pieces to a plate and set aside. Add the onions, garlic and aubergine to the roasting tin and toss them in the chicken cooking juices, drizzling with a little olive oil if extra lubrication seems necessary.

Return the chicken pieces to the vegetables in the tin and cook in the oven for a further 30 minutes, turning halfway through to ensure even browning. Add the courgettes, peas and parsley to the roasting tin for the final 8 minutes of cooking.

Pour 300 ml boiling water into a saucepan and place over high heat. Add the couscous and saffron and simmer for 5 minutes. Drain thoroughly, transfer to a large serving dish, season with salt and pepper and fluff up with a fork.

Arrange the cooked chicken and vegetables on top of the couscous, cover and keep warm. Use a metal spoon to skim off any excess fat from the roasting tin. Place on the stove and heat to simmering. Add 200 ml water, salt and pepper and boil for 4 minutes. Pour over the chicken and couscous and serve.

pad thai noodles

Pad Thai, probably the best known of all Thai noodle dishes, takes only five minutes to cook. Use thick ribbon-like rice noodles ('rice sticks') for authenticity, or rice vermicelli or egg noodles. Tamarind, commonly used in Asian cooking, has a unique sour flavour, but you can substitute freshly squeezed lime juice.

4 tablespoons sunflower oil

4 eggs, lightly beaten

150 g dried thick rice noodles, soaked in warm water for 5 minutes, then drained

100 g kale or other leafy greens, tough central core removed and leaves coarsely chopped

4 tablespoons tamarind paste or 2 tablespoons freshly squeezed lime juice

4 tablespoons sweet chilli sauce

4 tablespoons light soy sauce

1 large carrot, about 200 g, grated

100 g beansprouts

to serve

50 g roasted peanuts, chopped

4 spring onions, thinly sliced

coriander leaves

serves 4

Heat a wok until very hot, then add the oil. Add the eggs and noodles and stir-fry for about 2 minutes until the eggs are lightly scrambled. Add the remaining ingredients and stir-fry for a further 3–5 minutes until the noodles are cooked.

Divide between 4 warmed bowls and serve sprinkled with the peanuts, spring onions and coriander.

gingered chicken noodles

Most noodle dishes take just a matter of minutes to cook –
in fact, noodles made of rice flour or mung bean starch are
ready almost instantly. Wheat-based noodles take the most
time, but even then only about the same as regular pasta.

2 tablespoons rice wine, such as Chinese
Shaohsing or Japanese mirin

2 teaspoons cornflour

350 g skinless chicken breasts

175 g Chinese dried egg noodles

3 tablespoons peanut or sunflower oil

3 cm fresh ginger, peeled and thinly sliced

125 g mangetout, thinly sliced

4 tablespoons chopped fresh
garlic chives or chives

125 g cashew nuts, toasted in
a dry frying pan, then chopped

sauce

100 ml chicken stock

2 tablespoons dark soy sauce

1 tablespoon freshly squeezed lemon juice

1 tablespoon sesame oil

2 teaspoons soft brown sugar

serves 4

Put the rice wine and cornflour in a bowl and mix well. Cut the
chicken into small chunks, add to the bowl, stir well and set aside
to marinate while you prepare the remaining ingredients.

Soak the noodles according to the instructions on the packet,
then drain and shake dry.

Put all the sauce ingredients in a small bowl and mix well.

Heat half the oil in a wok or large frying pan, then add the
chicken and stir-fry for 2 minutes until golden. Remove to a plate
and wipe the pan clean. Add the remaining oil, then the ginger
and mangetout and fry for 1 minute. Return the chicken to
the pan, then add the noodles and sauce. Heat through for
2 minutes. Add the garlic chives and cashew nuts, stir well
and serve immediately.

Rice noodles cook very quickly, so be careful not to overcook them. Rinsing them in boiling water removes excess starch and keeps them in strands, not clumps.

warm thai crab rice noodles

250 g dried rice noodles, preferably thin

340 g canned white crabmeat, drained, or 200 g fresh

dressing

2 tablespoons sunflower oil

1 medium red chilli, finely chopped

1 medium green chilli, finely chopped

2.5 cm piece of fresh ginger, peeled and finely chopped

grated zest of 1 unwaxed lime and freshly squeezed juice of 2 limes

1 tablespoon Thai fish sauce

leaves from a large bunch of coriander

50 g cashew nuts, lightly toasted in a dry frying pan

sea salt and freshly ground black pepper

serves 4 as a starter or light lunch

Soak or cook the noodles as directed on the packet. Meanwhile, boil the kettle and put the crabmeat in a large bowl.

To make the dressing, put the oil in another bowl. Add the chillies, ginger, lime zest and juice, fish sauce and coriander. Stir, then add to the bowl of crabmeat. Add salt and pepper to taste.

When the noodles are cooked, drain and rinse with the boiling water from the kettle. Return the noodles to their bowl or saucepan, then add half the crab mixture and half the cashew nuts. Toss well.

Divide the noodles between 4 plates or bowls and top each with a spoonful of the remaining crab mixture. Sprinkle with the remaining nuts and serve.

paella

This wonderful Spanish dish is very easy to make and a joy to eat. Don't be put off by the long list of ingredients – they will all be readily available in your local supermarket. On special occasions, serve the paella with a mixed leaf salad, followed by fresh fruit and Spanish cheeses.

12 mussels

2 tablespoons olive oil

1 onion, finely chopped

2 garlic cloves, crushed and chopped

100 g chorizo sausage, thickly sliced

4 skinned chicken pieces, trimmed

200 g long-grain rice

a large pinch of saffron strands

600 ml chicken stock

250 ml white wine

8 large prawns

100 g squid, cleaned and cut into rings

2 lemons, the juice from 1 and the other cut into wedges

sea salt and freshly ground black pepper

a bunch of flat leaf parsley, chopped, to serve

serves 4

Scrub the mussels clean and rinse them in several changes of cold water to remove grit. Pull off the beards or seaweed-like threads and discard any mussels that are cracked or that don't close when tapped against the kitchen counter – these are dead and not edible.

Heat the olive oil in a paella pan or large frying pan. Add the onion, garlic and chorizo. Cook over low heat until the onion is softened and translucent, about 5 minutes. Add the chicken pieces and cook for about 5 minutes on each side until lightly browned.

Add the rice, saffron and stock to the pan and mix well. Bring the mixture to the boil, reduce the heat and simmer for 15 minutes, stirring so the rice doesn't stick to the base of the pan. Add more stock if needed.

Add the white wine, mussels, prawns, squid, salt and pepper. Cover with a lid or piece of foil and cook, without stirring, for a further 8–10 minutes. Stir the lemon juice into the paella. Top with the chopped parsley and serve from the pan with lemon wedges on the side.

puddings

plum fudge puddings

Even if you never make puddings at any other time, you probably do when you have people to dinner. Perfect for such an occasion, these little plum fudge puddings can be prepared well in advance, then cooked just before serving.

50 g unsalted butter

50 g honey

2 tablespoons double cream

2 tablespoons soft brown sugar

1 teaspoon ground mixed spice

75 g fresh white breadcrumbs

2 ripe plums, halved, stoned and thinly sliced

crème fraîche, to serve

4 ramekins, 150 ml each

a baking sheet

serves 4

Put the butter, honey and cream in a saucepan and heat until the butter is melted. Put the sugar, spice and breadcrumbs in a bowl and stir well.

Divide half the buttery fudge mixture between the ramekins and top with a layer of plum slices and half the breadcrumb mix. Add another layer of plums and top with the remaining breadcrumbs. Spoon over the remaining sauce.

Set on a baking sheet and bake in a preheated oven at 200°C (400°F) Gas 6 for 20 minutes. Remove from the oven and let cool for 5 minutes, then carefully unmould the puddings and serve with a spoonful of crème fraîche.

fresh figs
with vin santo and mascarpone

250 g mascarpone cheese

25–50 g icing sugar,
or to taste

6 tablespoons Vin Santo, plus
extra to serve

12 ripe figs

serves 6

This lovely, simple dish is best served when you can find very good-quality fresh figs. Vin Santo is an Italian sweet wine that marries well with the flavour of both the figs and the mascarpone. If you can't find it, you could use port or a cream sherry instead.

Put the mascarpone in a bowl, add the icing sugar and Vin Santo and beat until smooth. Set aside to infuse for 30 minutes, then transfer to a small serving bowl.

Cut the figs in half and arrange on a large serving platter with the bowl of mascarpone. Serve with the bottle of Vin Santo for guests to help themselves.

classic lemon tart

This is a tart filled with an uncooked lemon curd and baked in the oven until just firm. For a party you could make really tiny ones instead. If you are making bite-sized morsels, the pastry must be wonderfully thin so that they melt in the mouth.

1 recipe Sweet Rich Shortcrust Pastry (page 234)

1 egg, beaten, to seal the pastry

crème fraîche, to serve (optional)

lemon filling

6 large eggs

350 g caster sugar

finely grated zest and strained juice of 4 juicy unwaxed lemons

125 g unsalted butter, melted

a loose-based fluted tart tin, 23 cm diameter

foil or baking parchment and baking beans

a baking sheet

serves 8

Bring the pastry to room temperature.

Roll out the pastry thinly on a lightly floured work surface, and use to line the tart tin. Chill or freeze for 15 minutes. Line the case with a sheet of non-stick baking parchment, then fill with baking beans or dried beans. Set on a baking sheet and bake 'blind' in the centre of a preheated oven at 190°C (375°F) Gas 5 for 10–12 minutes, then carefully remove the paper and beans. Bake for a further 5–7 minutes to dry out completely.

Brush with beaten egg, then bake again for 5–10 minutes until set and shiny to prevent the filling from making the pastry soggy. Remove from the oven, then lower the temperature to 150°C (300°F) Gas 2.

To make the lemon filling, put the eggs, sugar, lemon zest and juice and butter in a food processor and blend until smooth.

Set the tart shell on a baking sheet and pour in the filling. Bake for about 1 hour (it may need a little longer, depending on your oven) until just set. Remove from the oven and let cool completely before serving. Serve at room temperature, with a spoonful of crème fraîche, if using.

A tart named after the sisters who, as legend has it, created an upside-down apple tart by mistake! The type of apple used is crucial here – it must retain its shape during cooking and yet have a good flavour. Try Cox's Orange Pippins, Golden Delicious or Jonagolds.

tarte des demoiselles tatin

450 g frozen puff pastry, thawed

300 g granulated sugar

150 g chilled unsalted butter, thinly sliced

2.25–2.5 kg evenly sized dessert apples, peeled, halved and cored

crème fraîche or whipped cream, to serve

non-stick baking parchment

a baking sheet

a flameproof cast-iron frying pan or tarte tatin dish, 28 cm diameter

serves 6

Roll out the pastry on non-stick baking parchment to a circle about 30 cm in diameter, slide onto a baking sheet and chill. Sprinkle the sugar over the base of the frying pan or tarte tatin dish. Cover with the sliced butter. Lay the apple halves around the outside of the pan. Set the first one at an angle, almost on its edge, then arrange the others so that they slightly overlap and butt up against each other. Add another ring of apples inside, then close the gap in the centre. The apples should cover the surface of the pan. They will look awkward and bulky, but will cook down and meld together later.

Put the pan over gentle heat and cook for about 45 minutes until the sugar and butter have caramelized and the apples have softened underneath. (Check from time to time and adjust the heat if necessary. The juices will gradually bubble up the sides; keep cooking until they are a dark amber.)

Lay the pastry over the apples in the pan and tuck the edges down into the pan, making the rim of the tart. Prick the top of the pastry here and there with a fork, then set the pan on the baking sheet. Bake in a preheated oven at 190°C (375°F) Gas 5 for 25–30 minutes until the pastry is risen and golden.

Remove the pan from the oven and immediately invert onto a warm serving plate. Remove any apple slices that have stuck to the pan and replace them in the tart. Serve warm, not hot, with crème fraîche or cream.

sticky chocolate pecan pie

180 g plain flour, plus extra for dusting

a pinch of salt

1 tablespoon caster sugar

115 g unsalted butter, chilled and cut into small pieces

1 large egg yolk mixed with 1 tablespoon cold water

vanilla ice cream or whipped cream, to serve

chocolate filling

45 g unsalted butter, softened

125 g light muscovado sugar

150 ml golden syrup

3 large eggs, beaten

1 teaspoon vanilla essence

100 g plain chocolate, melted

100 g pecan nuts

a loose-based flan tin, 23 cm diameter, well buttered

baking parchment and baking beans or dried beans

serves 8

Incredibly rich and gooey, this is a real treat. The crumbly pastry is simple to make in a food processor and the filling has a wonderfully fudgy taste and texture. Use a freshly opened packet of pecans for best results.

To make the pastry, put the flour, salt, sugar and butter in a food processor and process until the mixture resembles fine crumbs. With the machine running, add the egg yolk and water through the feed tube. Run the machine until the pastry comes together. If there are dry crumbs, add a teaspoon or so more water.

Put the pastry onto a floured work surface and, using a rolling pin, roll out to a large circle about 6 cm larger than the flan tin, then use to line the tin. Prick the base of the pastry case with a fork, then chill for 15 minutes.

Line the pastry case with a sheet of non-stick baking parchment, then fill with baking beans or dried beans. Bake 'blind' in a preheated oven at 180°C (350°F) Gas 4 for about 12 minutes, then carefully remove the paper and beans. Bake for a further 10 minutes until lightly golden and just firm. Remove from the oven and let cool while making the filling.

Put the butter, sugar and golden syrup in a bowl and, using a wooden spoon or electric mixer, beat until smooth. Gradually beat in the eggs and then the vanilla essence. Stir in the melted chocolate, followed by the pecan nuts.

Pour the mixture into the prepared pastry case and bake in a preheated oven at 180°C (350°F) Gas 4 for 35 minutes until just firm to the touch. Remove from the oven and let cool – the filling will sink slightly. Serve warm or at room temperature with vanilla ice cream or whipped cream. Best eaten within 4 days.

A delicious finale for a lovely summertime dinner, this very light cake is best served with piles of berries and whipped cream.

italian chocolate amaretto torta

110 g plain chocolate, chopped

2 tablespoons Amaretto liqueur

110 g unsalted butter,
at room temperature

110 g caster sugar, plus 1 tablespoon

3 large eggs, separated

60 g amaretti biscuits, crushed

60 g plain flour, sifted

icing sugar

to serve

whipped cream

blueberries or raspberries

*a loose-based sandwich tin,
20 cm diameter, buttered,
base-lined, then floured*

serves 8

Put the chocolate and Amaretto in a heatproof bowl set over a saucepan of steaming but not boiling water and leave until the chocolate has melted (do not let the base of the bowl touch the water). Remove the bowl from the heat, stir gently and let cool.

Put the butter and 110 g caster sugar in a bowl and, using a wooden spoon or electric mixer, beat until very light and fluffy. Beat in the egg yolks one at a time, then stir in the cooled chocolate. When thoroughly blended, use a large metal spoon to fold in the crushed biscuits and flour.

Put the egg whites in a spotlessly clean, grease-free bowl and, using an electric whisk or mixer, whisk until stiff peaks form. Whisk in 1 tablespoon caster sugar to make a stiff, glossy meringue, then fold into the cake mixture in 3 batches.

Transfer the mixture to the prepared tin and bake in a preheated oven at 180°C (350°F) Gas 4 for 30–35 minutes until just firm to the touch. Let cool in the tin for 10 minutes, then remove from the tin and transfer to a wire rack to cool completely.

Sprinkle with icing sugar and serve slightly warm or at room temperature with whipped cream and fresh berries. Best eaten within 3 days.

hot whisky pancakes
with raspberries

You can make these pancakes ahead of time – keep them in the refrigerator for up to two days, separated by squares of greaseproof paper. Alternatively, freeze them once they have cooled and remove from the freezer 30 minutes before using.

55 g plain flour
a pinch of salt
1 egg
150 ml milk
2 teaspoons peanut oil
300 ml freshly squeezed orange juice
2 tablespoons honey
15 g butter
3 tablespoons whisky
175 g fresh raspberries
icing sugar, to dust
cream or Greek yoghurt, to serve

serves 4

Sift the flour and salt into a large bowl. Make a well in the centre and crack the egg in. Gradually whisk in the milk to form a smooth batter.

Heat a medium non-stick frying pan. Add a little oil and wipe out with kitchen paper. Pour enough batter into the pan to coat the base, then cook for about 1 minute. Loosen the edges with a long-handled turner, flip the pancake and cook for 1 minute more. Transfer to a plate and repeat with the remaining mixture to make 3 more pancakes. Set aside.

Pour the orange juice into the frying pan and add the honey and butter. Bring to the boil, reduce the heat and simmer for 5 minutes to concentrate the flavours and thicken the sauce slightly. Stir in the whisky.

Carefully fold each pancake in half, then in half again to make a triangle, and slide them into the simmering sauce. Heat for 30 seconds to warm through.

Transfer the pancakes and sauce to a serving plate and sprinkle with raspberries. Dust lightly with icing sugar and serve with cream or Greek yoghurt.

romanov parfait

Strawberries Romanov is a classic French dish. This sundae version is elegant enough to grace any dinner party.

1 punnet strawberries, about 250 g

2 tablespoons liqueur, such as Cointreau, Grand Marnier or Curaçao

1½ tablespoons icing sugar

125 ml whipping cream

a few drops of vanilla essence

4–8 scoops strawberry or vanilla ice cream

4 sundae glasses

serves 4

Rinse the strawberries, pat dry with kitchen paper and reserve 4 for decoration. Hull and halve the remainder (always rinse before hulling, not after, or the strawberries will fill with water).

Put the halved berries in a bowl, sprinkle with the liqueur and 1 tablespoon of the icing sugar and set aside for 30 minutes.

Whip the cream with the vanilla and the remaining icing sugar until firm peaks form. Cover and chill until ready to use.

To serve, spoon the berries into sundae glasses and top with ice cream, whipped cream and a reserved strawberry, halved.

coconut ice cream

This subtle ice cream has only four
ingredients – five if you count the lime zest –
yet tastes heavenly. It is perfect for serving
after any Asian-style main course, such as
Green Thai Vegetable Curry (page 94).

500 ml milk

250 g caster sugar

500 ml unsweetened, canned
coconut milk

1 tablespoon dark rum
or fresh lime juice

unwaxed lime zest or wedges,
to serve

ice cream maker (optional)

serves 8

Put half the milk and all the sugar into a heavy-based
saucepan and bring to the boil, stirring until the sugar is
dissolved. Remove from the heat. Add the remaining milk
and the coconut milk. Cool over iced water and stir in the
rum or lime juice.

Transfer to an ice-cream making machine. Churn for
25–40 minutes, or according to the manufacturer's
instructions, until firm and silky. Alternatively, freeze in
plastic trays until the mixture is hard at the edges but
soft in the centre. Remove and stir well, then refreeze
as before. Repeat and refreeze.

Serve in bowls, glasses or cones, topped with strips
of lime zest or with lime wedges for squeezing.

party food
& drink

luxury hoummus

You can really taste the difference in homemade hoummus, especially this deluxe, caper-topped version.

Put the chickpeas, tahini paste and garlic in a food processor and blend until smooth. Add the lemon juice, with 3 tablespoons of the oil and 1 tablespoon boiling water. Process until very smooth. Add plenty of salt and pepper.

Put the parsley, capers, dried chillies and the remaining olive oil in a bowl and mix well.

Put a mound of the hoummus on each grilled pita bread and top with a spoonful of the parsley-caper mixture. Drizzle with olive oil and serve with lemon wedges.

400 g canned chickpeas, rinsed and drained

3 tablespoons tahini paste

2 garlic cloves, coarsely chopped

freshly squeezed juice of 1 lemon

4 tablespoons extra virgin olive oil, plus extra for drizzling

a large bunch of flat leaf parsley, coarsely chopped

2 tablespoons capers, rinsed and drained

½ teaspoon crushed dried chillies

sea salt and freshly ground black pepper

to serve

4 pita breads, grilled

1 lemon, cut into wedges

serves 4 as a starter

green olives with fennel

If you have fennel flowering in your garden, use the whole seed heads for this dish. Otherwise, use fennel seeds.

Pack most of the olives loosely into the sterilized jar(s) with tongs or a spoon.

Put the oil in a heavy-based saucepan and heat to 180°C (350°F) or until a small cube of bread turns golden brown in about 40 seconds.

Using a slotted spoon, lower the halved garlic heads and the fennel flower heads into the oil. Let them sizzle briefly, for about 30 seconds, then lift them out and add to or divide evenly between the jar(s). Scatter in the peppercorns, fennel seeds and cloves. Top up with the remaining olives.

Pour the sizzling hot oil carefully over the olives until covered. Let cool for about 2 minutes, then pour the remaining oil carefully into the jar(s) until completely filled. Let cool, uncovered and undisturbed. Seal tightly and store in a cool, dark cupboard until ready to serve.

500 g preserved green olives, washed and dried with kitchen paper, then pricked with a fork

500 ml extra virgin olive oil

2 whole heads of fresh garlic, halved crossways

4–8 fresh fennel flower heads, seeds intact (optional)

3 tablespoons black peppercorns, cracked or coarsely crushed

2 tablespoons fennel seeds

1 teaspoon cloves

1 litre jar or 2 x 500 ml jars, sterilized (page 4)

makes 1 large or 2 small jars

potato skins with green dip

You can have the cheese either melted and soft or crisp and crunchy – check as the skins cook and remove at the right moment. Save the potato middles for another day.

12 large baking potatoes

200 ml olive oil

400 g mature Cheddar cheese, grated

green dip

400 ml sour cream

2 bunches of chives, chopped

2 bunches of spring onions, chopped

a bunch of flat leaf parsley, chopped

sea salt and freshly ground black pepper

a baking sheet, lightly oiled

serves 24

Using a small, sharp knife, pierce each potato right through the middle. Bake in a preheated oven at 180°C (350°F) Gas 4 for 1 hour 10 minutes until completely cooked. Remove and set aside until cool enough to handle. Cut each potato in half lengthways and, using a dessertspoon, scoop out the soft potato middles, leaving a thin layer lining the skin. Cut each skin half into 4 wedges, then cover and chill until needed.

Brush oil over the potato skins and arrange in a single layer on the prepared baking sheet. Bake at the top of a preheated oven at 220°C (425°F) Gas 7 for 30 minutes until golden, moving the potatoes around occasionally to ensure even cooking. Remove from the oven and reduce the heat to 200°C (400°F) Gas 6. Sprinkle with cheese and return to the oven for 5–10 minutes, until the cheese is melted or crunchy, checking after 5 minutes if you want it melted.

To make the dip, put the sour cream, chives, spring onions and parsley in a bowl. Add salt and pepper to taste and mix well. Serve with the potato skins.

slow-roasted tomato and herb tartlets with feta

1 recipe Pâte Brisée (page 235)

slow-roasted tomatoes

12 large ripe cherry tomatoes

2 garlic cloves, finely chopped

1 tablespoon dried oregano

4 tablespoons olive oil

sea salt and freshly ground black pepper

herby cheese filling

80 g full-fat soft cheese with garlic and herbs (such as Boursin)

1 large egg, beaten

150 ml double cream

4 tablespoons chopped fresh mixed herbs (such as parsley, basil, marjoram or chives)

75 g feta cheese

tiny sprigs of thyme or cut chives, to finish

sea salt and freshly ground black pepper

a plain biscuit cutter, 6 cm diameter

2 mini muffin tins, 12 holes each

a baking sheet

foil or baking parchment and baking beans

makes 24 tartlets

Tiny tartlets are great to serve at a drinks party. These look stunning and have a secret pocket of feta cheese lurking in the creamy, herby filling underneath the tomatoes. Make double quantity of the tomatoes – they keep well in the refrigerator and are great in salads.

Preheat the oven to 200°C (400°F) Gas 6. Bring the pastry to room temperature, then roll out as thinly as possible on a lightly floured work surface. Use the biscuit cutter to stamp out 24 circles. Line the muffin tins with the pastry circles, then prick the bases and chill or freeze for 15 minutes. Bake blind following the method on page 203, then remove from the tins and let cool. (The cases will keep for up to 1 week in an airtight tin, but reheat to crisp before filling.)

Turn the oven down to 160°C (325°F) Gas 3. Cut the tomatoes in half around the middle. Arrange cut side up on a baking sheet. Put the garlic, oregano, oil and lots of pepper in a bowl and mix well, then spoon or brush over the cut tomatoes. Bake slowly in the oven for 1½–2 hours, checking every now and then. They should be slightly shrunk and still a brilliant red colour – if too dark, they will taste bitter.

Put the soft cheese in a bowl, add the egg, cream and chopped herbs and beat until smooth. Season well. Cut the feta into 24 small cubes that will fit inside the pastry cases. When ready to bake, set the cases on a baking sheet, put a cube of feta in each one and top up with the garlic and herb mixture. Bake in a preheated oven at 180°C (350°F) Gas 4 for 15–20 minutes or until the filling is set. Top each with a tomato half, a sprinkle of the cooking juices and a thyme sprig or chive stem. Serve warm.

miniature spring rolls

Spring rolls should be lean, crisp and refreshing and make effortless party snacks. Serve them with your favourite dipping sauces, such as chilli sauce or soy sauce.

125 g fresh beansprouts

75 g spring onions, thinly sliced

75 g carrots, thinly sliced

75 g bamboo shoots, fresh or soaked, thinly sliced

75 g fresh shiitake mushrooms, stems discarded, caps thinly sliced

5 cm piece fresh ginger, thinly sliced

3 tablespoons peanut oil, plus extra for frying

50 g firm beancurd (tofu), finely diced

2 teaspoons caster sugar

1 tablespoon light soy sauce

1 tablespoon Chinese rice wine or dry sherry

20 spring roll wrappers or wonton skins

2 tablespoons flour

2 tablespoons water

makes 40

Blanch the beansprouts for 1 minute in boiling water, then refresh in iced water. Top and tail them, discarding the ends. Put in a bowl, add the other vegetables and the ginger and mix gently.

Heat the 3 tablespoons oil, add the vegetables and stir-fry for 1–1½ minutes. Add the beancurd, sugar, soy sauce and rice wine or sherry, then cook for 1 minute longer. Let cool, then divide into 8 portions (each will be enough for 5 spring rolls).

Cut each wrapper in half diagonally. Put 1 portion of filling onto the long side, a third of the way from the edge. Fold the long side over the filling, then fold over the side flaps. Roll up. Mix the flour and water and dab a little of the mixture on the loose end of the roll. Press to seal. Set the rolls on a lightly floured surface, not touching, until all are made.

Heat the oil to 190°C (375°F) or a little hotter, but do not let it smoke. Deep-fry the rolls, 8–10 at a time, for 3–4 minutes. Remove with a wire strainer, drain on crumpled kitchen paper and keep warm in a low oven. Let the oil reheat before cooking the next batch.

When all the spring rolls have been cooked, serve with your choice of dips.

baby pizzas

500 g unbleached plain flour

2 sachets easy-blend dried yeast, 7 g each

1 teaspoon salt

4 tablespoons extra virgin olive oil

toppings

250 ml fresh tomato sauce, tapenade or
sun-dried tomato pesto

250 ml sautéed spinach, rocket or roasted peppers

100 g black olives and/or capers

50 g anchovies, halved lengthways
and/or toasted pine nuts

8 garlic cloves, chopped

1–2 tablespoons chopped fresh rosemary,
sage or thyme

250 g mozzarella cheese, drained and cubed

250 ml extra virgin olive oil

sea salt and freshly ground black pepper

2 baking sheets, lightly oiled
a round biscuit cutter, 5–7.5 cm diameter

makes 32–40

There's nothing better for a party than homemade mini pizzas. They are incredibly easy to make – all you need is a food processor – and your guests will be able to try lots of different toppings.

To make the dough, put the flour, yeast and salt in a food processor. Pulse briefly to sift the dry ingredients. Add the olive oil and 360 ml lukewarm water. Process in short bursts for 15 seconds to form a soft mass, not a ball.

Turn out onto a floured work surface and knead by hand for 2 minutes, slamming down the dough 2–3 times to help develop the gluten. Put the dough in a clean, oiled bowl. Turn it over once to coat with oil. Put the bowl of dough into a large plastic bag, seal and let rise until doubled in size, about 1½ hours.

Put the dough onto the work surface and punch it down with oiled hands. Cut in half. Pat and roll out each piece to a circle about 5 mm thick. Push dimples all over it with your fingers.

Using the biscuit cutter, cut out about 16 small discs. Set them on a baking sheet. Top each one with ½–1 teaspoon sauce, tapenade or pesto. Add spinach, rocket or roasted peppers, then a choice of olives, capers, anchovies or pine nuts. Add garlic, herbs or cheese. Season to taste and sprinkle with olive oil. Repeat, using the second half of the dough on a second baking sheet.

Set aside for 15–20 minutes, then bake at 240°C (475°F) Gas 9 for 12–15 minutes or until the bases are blistered and crisp, the toppings aromatic and the cheese melted. Serve hot.

pimm's

1 part Pimm's

3 parts ginger ale, lemonade or soda

borage flowers

curls of cucumber peel

sliced lemons

sprigs of mint

serves from 1 to a party

This traditional English summertime drink is perfect for parties. When borage is in flower, freeze the pretty blue blossoms in ice cubes for out-of-season Pimm's drinks. Allow 240 ml per drink, and at least two drinks per person – but be prepared for repeat orders!

Put all the ingredients in a jug of ice, stir and serve.

champagne cocktails

The ultimate party drink, champagne is always
a great hit and these cocktails are delicious. You
could use another sparkling wine, if you preferred.

1 teaspoon of a liqueur such as
Poire William, peach or
strawberry liqueur, framboise,
Midori, blue curaçao or
Galliano and the pulp of
1 passionfruit

alternatively, 4 tablespoons of
fruit juice, such as pear,
pineapple, peach or apricot

champagne

serves 1

Put liqueur or fruit juice in a champagne flute
or coupé and top with champagne.

sea breeze

This is a modern, thirst-quenching variation on the classic Screwdriver. Any combination of vodka and freshly squeezed juices will work in creating a Breeze to suit your personal taste.

50 ml vodka
cranberry juice
fresh grapefruit juice
1 lime wedge
serves 1

Pour a large shot of vodka into a highball glass filled with ice. Three-quarters fill the glass with cranberry juice and top with fresh grapefruit juice. Garnish with a lime wedge and serve with a straw.

mint mojito

Zesty and refreshing, a Mojito is the perfect summer drink to refresh and revive. Before serving, strain through a fine-mesh sieve to remove all the pieces of chopped mint (it's the mint juice that gives it such an amazing colour).

Put the rum, lime juice, sugar or sugar syrup, mint leaves and ice cubes in a blender, zap well, then strain into a glass half-filled with ice. Serve straight or topped up with sparkling mineral water, with a sprig of mint and a curl of lime zest.

60 ml white rum

freshly squeezed juice of 1 lime

1 tablespoon sugar syrup or caster sugar

leaves from a large bunch of mint

ice cubes

sparkling mineral water (optional)

mint sprigs and lime zest, to serve

serves 1

margarita

The usual way of serving margaritas is to rim the glass with salt. This is optional, but a twist of lime is absolutely crucial! Some people like to add a dash of sugar, though this may depend on the flavour of the limes.

1 part tequila

1 part triple sec or other orange liqueur, such as Cointreau

2 parts fresh lime juice, thinned with water if preferred

crushed ice or ice cubes

a twist of lime, to serve

serves 1

Shake or blend the tequila, triple sec, lime juice and crushed ice or ice cubes. Pour into a salt-rimmed glass, if liked, and serve with a twist of lime.

Variations

Frozen Margarita

In a blender, whizz 1 part tequila, 1 part Grand Marnier, 2 parts fresh lime juice, 2 parts ice and sugar to taste, then pour into an ice-frosted, salt-rimmed glass.

Cranberry Margarita

In a blender, whizz 1 part each of tequila, Cointreau and lime juice with 2 parts of cranberry juice, plus ice and sugar to taste. Serve immediately.

pastry basics

sweet rich shortcrust pastry

This is a wonderfully light and crumbly pastry. It is best used for richer pies and tarts, or where the shell is more than just a carrier for the filling and the taste of the pastry is important.

250 g plain flour

½ teaspoon salt

2 tablespoons icing sugar

125 g unsalted butter, chilled and diced

2 medium egg yolks

2 tablespoons iced water

makes about 400 g pastry

Put the flour, salt and icing sugar in a food processor, add the butter and blend until the mixture looks like fine breadcrumbs. Mix the egg yolk with the iced water and add to the machine. Blend again until it begins to form a ball. Add another tablespoon of water if it is too dry and blend again.

Tip out onto a floured work surface and knead lightly until smooth, then shape into a flattened ball. Wrap in clingfilm and chill for 30 minutes before rolling.

250 g plain flour

1 teaspoon salt

125 g unsalted butter, softened

1 large egg yolk

2½–3 tablespoons iced water

makes about 350 g pastry

pâte brisée

This pastry has a fine texture and should be rolled out thinly – to about 3 mm. Don't be tempted to leave out the water – it makes the pastry stronger and easier to handle in the end.

Sift the flour and salt together onto a sheet of greaseproof paper.

Put the butter and egg yolk in a food processor and blend until smooth. Add the water and blend again. Add the flour and salt and pulse until just mixed.

Transfer to a lightly floured work surface and knead gently until smooth. Form into a ball, flatten slightly and wrap in clingfilm. Chill in the refrigerator for at least 30 minutes.

Let the dough return to room temperature before rolling out.

index

credits

Photographs

Peter Cassidy Pages 3l, 3r, 9al, 16, 20, 25al, bl, bc & br, 27, 32–33, 35, 36, 39, 43ac, ar & bl, 47, 53, 54, 57cl, 58, 61, 69, 76, 77, 78, 80, 81al, ac, ar & c, 95, 103, 108, 111ar, cr, br, bc & bl, 113, 114, 116, 119, 123, 127, 129, 132, 133al, ac & ar, 135, 136, 140, 144, 148, 150, 151al, ac, br, bl & cl, 153, 154, 157, 162, 165, 170, 172, 175cl & bl, 176, 179, 190, 193, 197al, ar, br, bl & cl, 198, 210, 217br, 218, 219, 227

Debi Treloar Endpapers, pages 1, 2, 3cl, 6, 7, 8, 9ac, c & br, 25ar, 56, 57bl, bc & br, 70, 73, 74, 111al, 120, 133bl, 143, 151ar, 161, 169, 175ar & bc, 183, 186, 194, 213, 216, 217 all above & bl, 220

William Lingwood Pages 21, 31, 40–41, 43cr, 83, 86, 87, 98, 102, 112, 117, 130, 138–139, 149, 158–159, 174, 175al & br, 180, 184–185, 203, 228, 229, 230, 231, 234, 236–239

Philip Webb Pages 11, 28–29, 44–45, 48–49, 50, 65, 66, 81br, 91, 92, 99, 100, 104–105, 107, 189

Ian Wallace Pages 9ar, 12, 14, 15, 19, 22, 57ar, 124, 133br, 147, 166, 201, 240

Martin Brigdale Pages 81bl, 96, 202, 205, 206, 209, 223, 235

David Brittain Page 3 background, 25c, 57al, 217cl

Jean Cazals Pages 62, 81bc, 82, 88

Craig Robertson Pages 52, 85, 97, 200

Jeremy Hopley Pages 42, 214, 224

David Montgomery Pages 141, 196, 197ac

Gus Filgate Page 24, 30

David Loftus Pages 5, 133cl

Caroline Arber Page 26

Henry Bourne Page 4

Dan Duchars Page 9bl

Tom Leighton Page 43br

James Merrell Page 233

Pia Tryde Page 110

Simon Walton Page 43al

Francesca Yorke Page 3cr

Recipes

CELIA BROOKS BROWN
American pancakes
Lemon potato latkes with gingered avocado crème
Celeriac, saffron and orange soup
Shiitake and field mushroom soup with madeira and thyme
Mexican gazpacho
Caesar salad
Warm chickpea salad
Pumpkin and tofu laksa
Roasted teriyaki tofu steaks
Minted char-grilled courgettes
Chilli greens with garlic crisps
Provençal roasted vegetables
Lemon-roasted baby potatoes
Pad Thai noodles

MAXINE CLARK
Smoked salmon and lemon pepper cream crostini
Roquefort tart with walnut and toasted garlic dressing
Classic lemon tart
Tarte Tatin
Slow-roasted tomato and herb tartlets with feta
Sweet rich shortcrust pastry
Pâte brisée

LINDA COLLISTER
Italian chocolate amaretto torta
Sticky chocolate pecan pie

CLARE FERGUSON
Prawns with parsley and lemon
Bresaola and rocket with olive oil and Parmesan
Spicy Thai chicken soup
Fresh green salad
Warm chicken and chorizo salad
Catalan spinach
Stir-fried chicken with greens
Boeuf en daube
Sicilian spaghetti
Coconut ice cream
Green olives with fennel
Miniature spring rolls
Baby pizzas

SILVANO FRANCO
Herbed tagliatelle with prawn skewers
Classic lasagne

MANISHA GAMBHIR HARKINS
Butternut squash soup with allspice and pine nuts
Andalusian chickpea soup with chorizo, paprika and saffron
Mozzarella, tomato and basil salad
Baked aubergine and tomato stacks
Chickpea and tomato masala with beans and coriander
Italian pork tenderloin with fennel and garlic
Burmese pork hinleh

ELSA PETERSEN-SCHEPELERN
Grilled polenta with grilled peppers
Pan-grilled Vietnamese beef with sweet potatoes, crème fraîche and chilli tomato relish
Romanov Parfait
Pimm's
Champagne cocktail
Mint mojito
Margarita

LOUISE PICKFORD
Waffles with maple syrup ice cream
Pecan and chocolate muffins
Scrambled eggs with mushrooms
Eggs benedict
Warm potato tortilla with smoked salmon
Baked chèvre
Lobster and fennel salad
Seared scallops with crushed potatoes
Peppered tuna steak with salsa rossa
Pan-fried chicken with creamy beans and leeks
Garlic roasted poussins
Chicken 'panini'
Steak with blue cheese butter
Pasta with melted ricotta and herby Parmesan sauce
Gingered chicken noodles
Plum fudge puddings
Fresh figs with Vin Santo and mascarpone

BEN REED
Sea Breeze

FIONA SMITH
Peking-style duck pancake wraps

SONIA STEVENSON
Provençal tian
North African charred vegetables
Traditional fish pie
Coq au vin
Braised lamb shanks with orange and marmalade

FRAN WARDE
Seared tuna salad with lime and soy dressing
Roasted aubergine and Parma ham salad
Chicken liver salad
Roasted salmon wrapped in prosciutto
Korean chicken
Roasted pheasant breasts with bacon, shallots and mushrooms
Steak and mushroom pie
Chicken and asparagus spaghetti
Coucous with roasted chicken and vegetables
Paella
Potato skins with green dip

LESLEY WATERS
French toast with smoky bacon and spiked tomatoes
Trout fishcakes
Chicory and radicchio salad with walnut dressing
Seared peppered beef salad with horseradish dressing
Green Thai vegetable curry
Classic creamy mashed potato
Steamed mussels with garlic and vermouth in a foil parcel
Hot wok chilli prawns
Salmon tempura
Seared swordfish with avocado salsa
Saffron fish roast
Mediterranean fish stew
Hot chicken tikka platter with yoghurt
Honeyed duck with mango salsa
Gremolata pork with lemon spinach
Venison sausages with port and cranberry ragout
Moroccan lamb tagine
Warm Thai crab rice noodles
Hot whisky pancakes with raspberries
Luxury hoummus